*This book is dedicated
to my wife Frances.*

Sell Anything By Mail!

FIRST CLASS

Sell Anything By Mail!

Frank Jefkins

BScEcon., BA(Hons), MCAM, ABC, FAIE, FIPR, FLCC, FInstSMM, MCIM

BOB ADAMS, INC.
PUBLISHERS

Holbrook, Massachusetts

Published by Bob Adams, Inc.
260 Center Street
Holbrook, Massachusetts 02343

Printed in the United States of America

ISBN: 1-55850-942-9

10 9 8 7 6 5 4 3 2 1

Originally published in the United Kingdom by Heinemann Professional Publishing.

Frank Jefkins can show you how to sell anything by mail.

Frank Jefkins has supplied direct response techniques to his own business for over twenty years, selling books and a variety of training courses worldwide. His mail order book service has customers in seventy countries, and his school has attracted management participants from forty-two countries since 1980. He has also worked as a copywriter for direct mail houses, and for several years produced direct mail pieces to sell advertising space in magazines. He has over twenty books in print, including the *International Dictionary of Marketing and Communication.*

Contents

Preface / 11

Chapter One: How to Avoid Junk Mail / 13

Chapter Two: Three Secrets of Successful Direct Response Marketing / 23

Chapter Three: How to Write Sales Letters / 39

Chapter Four: How to Compile and Ensure Good Mailing Lists / 51

Chapter Five: Insertions / 67

Chapter Six: One-piece Mailers / 71

Chapter Seven: How to Control Costs / 77

Chapter Eight: Envelopes / 85

Chapter Nine: Contents of a Mailing / 91

Chapter Ten: Catalogues / 99

Chapter Eleven: Working with the Printer and Typographer / 103

Chapter Twelve: Working with the Photographer / 111

Chapter Thirteen: Off-the-Page and Inserts / 117

Chapter Fourteen: How to Research and Record Results / 127

Appendices: List Brokers, Bibliography

Preface

Direct response marketing is big business. I have used it myself over the past 20 years to promote four businesses, both nationally and internationally.

Advertising is often criticized, direct mail is frequently maligned, and door-to-door distribution sometimes evokes contempt.

This book is not just a textbook laying down the rules. It criticizes the abuses of direct marketing that make it hard for you to succeed. At the same time, it invites you to decide how direct marketing can be applied profitably to your business.

How can you invest in economical and successful direct marketing? This book provides the answer. You may not always agree with what is said, but *Sell Anything By Mail* will make you think more critically about what is (and isn't) most likely to work for you.

Chapter One

How to Avoid Junk Mail

What is junk mail?

Some people regard it as any unsolicited commercial mail. They probably don't like any kind of advertising, and pretend it never influences them to buy anything. Without advertising, modern industrial society would not exist. Without advertising, we would be back to a feudal age of market stalls, small shops, small towns, and no factories.

As a direct-response manager at a major charitable organization recently put it, "Unprofitable mailings are junk, and profitable mailings are not. It really is as simple as that."

Is there really a reservoir of ill will toward direct mail marketing itself? Most of the fuss stems from the fact that harassed recipients of unwanted pieces often find it extremely difficult to get themselves off mailing lists. (One proven way is to write 'deceased' on the envelope and return it to sender.)

The foot-in-the-door salesperson of yesteryear has become today's persuasive letterbox marketer. With some one billion direct mail items being mailed yearly at a cost of $350 million, and an annual increase of 20%, it is not surprising that there is a lot of junk mail out there. This is a formidable torrent of advertising.

Advertising is said to reflect the economic prosperity of a country, so perhaps the increasing reliance on direct mail indicates an optimistic upturn. It also shows a more economic use of advertising—that is, less costly and better targeted ad campaigns.

Consumers are always critical of advertising, especially when it is thrust under their noses, as direct mail pieces and doorstoppers certainly are. You don't *have* to read press advertisements or posters; you can go to the kitchen for a snack when the commercials come on. But the direct mail piece is there on the front step or on your desk, demanding action of some sort. Can its very power and presence be its own undoing?

Some companies have not been very clever when offering their supposedly "limited" special offers, mailing the same person repeatedly. I mentioned this in the following letter (recently published in an industry trade publication) about one of the main causes of repetitive junk mail: careless keying of computer keyboards.

Dear Sir:

Direct mail often earns the name of junk mail simply because its mailing list creators are careless.

Every morning I receive direct mail advertisements that only contribute to the bulk of my dustbin contents. Yet I have run a successful business for 20 years that has been dependent on direct mail.

One of the secrets of my success has been that I never use an outside service.

During the past four weeks I have received some 20 offers of the Sun Life 'limited' bond! They must have wasted a fortune on mis-mailings. Shoals of begging letters have arrived. This week two firms have written to me as Mr. Jeffs, and Kompass has sent me two pieces, one addressed to Jepkins and the other to Jepherson. An insurance broker has mailed me in triplicate.

The reason for all these multiple mailings is that I have been addressed as Jenkins, Jeffrey, Jeffreys, Jeffery, Jeffries, Jephkins, Jepkins, Jifkins, and numerous other variations, which must defy deduplication efforts.

Yet, presumably, my personal name or business name has been taken from share registers, membership lists, directories, and other sources—where it appears correctly. Slovenly keyboarding is the culprit. List compilers and list brokers are the creators of junk mail.

To the list of culprits must be added those blanket mailers to whom it never occurs that someone who has been a member or customer for years finds it irritating to be repeatedly mailed as a new prospect. Among the worst antagonizers is American Express, a firm that seems to be ignorant of the identity of its cardholders.

Frank Jefkins

What is one to make of the following piece (generated in England) from one of the most inept mailers, American Express?

American Express Europe Limited
Card Services
P.O. Box 68
Amex House, Edward Street
Brighton, England BN2 1YL

Ms. Janet Pigott
Frank Jenkins School of Pub Re
84 Ballerds Way
Croydon
CR2 7LA

What attracts the better type of customer?
The better type of Card.

Dear Ms. Pigott,

If I asked you to describe your ideal customer, who would it be?
Someone with more money to spend than the average person? Who
spends more than most customers on hardback and paperback books?
And someone with no pre-set limit on how much they spend in your
bookstore?

I have a simple suggestion that could attract one million
customers like this into your store. Accept this invitation to
welcome American Express Cardmembers into your store and enjoy
increased sales.

American Express Cardmembers earn more

By accepting the American Express Card you'll be
welcoming one million Cardmembers who earn twice as much

*National
average income
£10,740*

as most people in the UK. Average UK
earnings are £10,740 ... Amex
Cardmembers earn on average
£25,000.

*Cardmember
average income
£25,000*

And they spend more too

You should make an average sale of £30 worth of books
to American Express Cardmembers. That's much more
than other customers spend.

What's more, American Express Cardmembers are keen
booklovers - and they closely match the typical book
buyer profile. In fact they could be just the type
of customer you'd like to see browsing in your store.

As you know, books are usually impulse buys - which is
another reason why it pays to accept the American
Express Card. Because 35% of Cardmembers'
purchases are bought on impulse. And
when it comes to choosing
the latest best-selling
paperbacks, glossy reference

*Average Card
transaction on
books £30*

books and hardbacks as gifts for family and
friends, the American Express Card has no
pre-set spending limit. This gives Cardmembers
extra financial freedom to choose just what they want.

*35% of all retail
purchases are impulse buys*

The sign that says 'Hello' to over 1,000,000 UK customers

In the UK alone over 1,000,000 people carry, and choose to pay with
the American Express Card.

In fact research has shown that Cardmembers prefer to shop where
they see the American Express 'Cards Welcome' sign.

The majority of our Cardmembers are aged between 25 and 45 - so you'll see why this represents a large market of young, free spending customers for you to profit from.

Say hello to thousands of wealthy overseas visitors too

American Express have 27 million Cardmembers Worldwide, and many of them frequently travel overseas - so accepting the American Express Card could represent an important source of potential new customers for you.

We encourage spending through national advertising

Throughout the world American Express spend heavily on encouraging our Cardmembers to use the Card whenever they make a purchase. This includes active support programmes for outlets like yours to help bring more profits your way. So when you welcome the American Express Card, you'll benefit from high spending Cardmembers who are constantly reminded of the benefits of using the Card.

A high percentage of foreign spending is charged to the American Express Card.

Accept our invitation to welcome the Card

When you choose to accept the Card, our Cardmembers will be looking out for the familiar white and blue sign. We'll supply you with these in addition to imprinters, decals and all the stationery your size of business requires.

And if you haven't considered welcoming the American Express Card into your

78% of all Cardmembers look for the 'Cards Welcome' sign

Over one million people carry the Card in the UK.

store before, you may have some questions you'd like to ask. That's why I'd like to invite you to accept our free consultation. Simply complete and return the enclosed reply card. Your local area manager will arrange a convenient time to see you. Accept a better card and open your store to <u>over 1 million</u> 'better types' of customer by returning the reply card today.

Yours sincerely

John Petersen

PS Remember, every day, high spending customers could be passing your store by because you don't accept the American Express Card - don't waste anymore time - reply today.

Let's begin by analyzing that puzzling address.

```
Ms Janet Pigott
Frank Jenkins School of Pub Re
84 Ballerds Way
Croydon CR2 7LA
```

There is no such person as Janet Pigott. The name is Jefkins, not Jenkins. And what is 'Pub Re'? The street is spelled "Ballards," not "Ballerds." The town is South Croydon, which meant that the post office had to write "South" on the envelope and transfer the letter to another sorting office.

Perhaps all that was intended was to arouse curiosity and get the letter opened, which of course it did. The personalized letter, directed to the non-existent Ms. Piggott, addressed her as if she was running a bookshop and should welcome American Express Cardmembers. The School does not have a bookshop (instead, it offers courses), and the four-page pictorial letter about booklovers and "your store" was irrelevant.

How does a large organization that is a major user of direct response mailings get so many things wrong at once?

The answer seems to have something to do with the size of the mailings in question. Maybe a half-million piece mailing can actually do the job just as effectively as a million-and-a-half-piece mailing . . . and less expensively. In other words, it may be a more successful and cheaper medium if there is a lot less of it!

Make no mistake: direct response marketing does work wonders. It all depends on how you do it. The great mail order houses have been running successful campaigns for more than a century. I have run a successful international business for 20 years using direct mail. I could not have done it with press advertising. Three reasons for its success have been a one-piece mailer; limited and selective mailing lists compiled in-house; and careful timing. None of these elementary techniques is applied by the junk mailers.

Public relations suffers from its own form of junk mail, resulting in an adversarial situation between media people and those who want coverage. Editors are inundated not only by badly written press releases, but by ones that have been wrongly timed or misdirected by lazy and unskilled compilation of mailing lists.

The principles of direct mail apply to news releases, but a lot of PR people are ignorant of them. As a result, they indulge in the blanket mailing of garbage. If out of 100 news releases only one is published, that is a hit rate of one percent. But if one release is sent to the only journal likely to publish it, and that journal does, that is a hit rate of 100 percent. The junk mail consists of the irrelevant 99 releases.

That is why the careful selection or culling of lists is so vital in direct response marketing. The problem is that sometimes one cannot know which names to eliminate. Even some of those who complain about junk mail may in fact prove to be customers in the long run.

Since there is no doubt about the success of direct mail, in both its effectiveness and its economy, we must consider carefully all the many techniques available. Junk mail results from the wrong use of techniques, and while it is impossible to placate the determined critic, many of the complaints and condemnations are avoidable. At least, you can try to avoid them.

So which methods are most likely to work for you? Which are the least likely to evoke the contemptuous dismissal of your pieces as junk mail? You will probably find that if the wrong technique is used it will be resented, but the right one will be welcomed and responded to.

The irony of direct response marketing is that some of it is too clever by half. But which half? Send a man a superb holiday brochure when he has just received his Christmas bonus and he will love you. Mail it when he has already spent his bonus and he will hate you. Or perhaps you think your timing is perfect on a given campaign—but the postal service's timing isn't.

Similarly, it may be a good idea to provoke action through something like a "jackpot" scratch card, which appeals to curiosity and greed. But if some mystery offer is sealed inside a complicated piece, and perforated edges have to be ripped off, the recipient may find this tiresome and toss it away, muttering "The hell with this." Reactions have to be anticipated—and better still, tested.

There are gimmicks galore in direct marketing, as we'll see later in this book. Some of them are marvelous; some are a damned nuisance.

Direct marketing, then, is full of opportunities—if you use your head. You don't just stuff things in envelopes and dump your efforts into the mailbox. Remember, there is a major public relations element in direct mail; it can make or break the perceived image of your organization. An image cannot be created, only deserved. Junk mail, however, can destroy a good reputation.

It comes down to simple planning, and to the definition of policy about your style of mailing. You need to be consistent, and consistency can exploit that secret of all successful advertising—*repetition*. Your style—the design of your envelopes, letterheads, order forms, leaflets, catalogues—should characterize your firm. Stick to it, and people will stick to you. This style can be your *corporate identity*, like that of a department store, oil company, car manufacturer, brewer, or airline—all instantly recognizable by their logo, colors, typography, or vehicles.

There are five basic rules to planning a direct marketing campaign:

1. *Identify your market.* What customers will you target? This can vary from one product or service to another.

2. *Determine the kind of response you are seeking.* An order with cash? An order against an invoice? A written inquiry? A telephone call? A visit to a supplier?

3. *Have a good reason for provoking response.* Is it the originality or topicality of the offer? The value for money? The quality of the product? There must be a good, clear reason for your target group to respond. No why, no buy!

4. *Determine the location of your market.* Is it local, regional, national, or international? What effect does this have on, say, prices, payments, guarantees, refunds, and delivery times?

5. *Determine proper timing.* There are often times you must work around: weekends and holidays; seasonal "rush" periods; and, with overseas mailings, periods like Ramadan in Muslim countries. With foreign mailings you will also have to consider how long it will take mail to reach its destination. Some places can be reached in days, others in weeks. Will you rely on the postal system, or use a commercial service? Of course, the category you choose for your mail will affect delivery. Similarly, some door-to-door distributions can be completed in three days, others in two weeks, according to the distributor.

For magazine promotions or inserts, you will have to book issues for future dates, often months ahead of time, but your ability to service orders will have to match insertion dates. Timing decisions must take into account your production of promotional material, how long it will take prospects to receive your message, your own purchase and receipt of merchandise, and the time it takes you to receive and fulfill orders.

If these five rules are obeyed, a good deal of junk mail can be avoided. Whether or not it is junk mail will be the decision of the receiver. Junk mail is a little like a garden weed: a plant where it shouldn't be, even if it's an orchid. Most of the "weeds" that make a garden untidy are delightful "wild flowers" when they grow in the countryside. Thus, what is junk mail for some is a pleasure and a benefit for others. Can you figure out who are the unwanted "some," and who are the desirable "others"?

Chapter Two

Three Secrets of Successful Direct Response Marketing

The three essentials of successful direct response marketing are:

1. A good offer.

2. A good mail piece.

3. A good mailing list.

Some experts amend this order by saying that the list followed by the offer are the two most vital variables in direct response marketing. The development of in-house customer or outside specialized databases, however, has contributed enormously to the efficiency of the mailing list. Of course, lists need to be culled and corrected regularly. Inefficient databases or misuse of them can also contribute to junk mail.

Returning to the three essentials in the order given above, let's consider the importance of the offer itself.

A GOOD OFFER

A good offer hinges on the marketer's knowledge of what the consumer is likely to buy, and the ability to purchase the right merchandise at the right price. The two are interdependent. Do you know your customers' needs, do you judge by the take-up of previous offers, or do you research the market?

Research can take many simple forms. The following are some suggested research techniques:

1. *Sample Mailings*. This method is a test market device which you design to estimate your offer's sales potential. Set a desired percentage of acceptances, and, if that percentage is achieved or exceeded, you can move on to broad-scale marketing. If the result is a flop you can drop the idea and try something else. This sort of testing can also be done with mailings themselves, or prices, to arrive at the one most likely to succeed. There are psychological attitudes to copy content, presentation, postage cost and price. A change in any one of these factors can make an offer more or less acceptable. Research can help you determine the best approach, so your mailing will be profitable.

2. *Primary Market Assessment*. You can study what is currently available on the market. Is something obviously popular and in demand—that you can supply? Conversely, is something unavailable? Can something fill an obvious want? Think back; remember some of the novel things now being sold that no one was previously supplying.

3. *Competitor Analysis*. Other people's offers are worth analyzing to see whether you can offer something different.

4. *Trade Magazines*. Editorials and advertisements may suggest goods, manufacturers, or importers that can be useful to you.

5. *Industrial Publications*. Visits to exhibitions and trade fairs may reveal merchandise you can handle. Trade magazines, in their editorials and advertise-

ments, may suggest goods, manufacturers or importers that can be useful to you.

One way or another, by keeping your eyes open and exploiting opportunities, you can find or create original, interesting offers of value to your customers and profit to you.

Be explicit

Armchair shopping allows prospective customers to have the shop virtually brought into their living room. It makes sense, then, that they should be given almost as much information as they would get from a face-to-face meeting with a salesperson. Their confidence in the products you market relies on this. Doubts must not emerge as a result of inadequate and unconvincing copy or illustrations.

It pays to analyze exactly what information the recipients of your mailing are likely to need. They probably won't go to the trouble of writing to you or calling you about details you have omitted.

This is not always easy to do. You know all about the merchandise or service; the recipient has never heard of it before. Bridging this communications gap is a skill you have to learn. Make sure you have given all the facts and explanations the reader needs to understand your offer.

The key to this is to keep things simple. One guaranteed way to bewilder a prospect is to spread the message over many pieces of paper instead of presenting the essential message in a compact, simple-to-understand format. Sometimes an envelope can be full of so many items that the reader does not know what to look at first and then, in desperation, discards the entire package.

For instance, a recent mailing by a major investment organization incorporated eight pieces of paper of various sizes, plus a business reply envelope. The contents?

1. A long letter on company stationery, printed on both sides of two odd-shaped unattached sheets. (This repeated much of the material outlined elsewhere, yet lacked certain vital information.)

2. A large three-color proposal form which purported to answer all your questions. (But didn't.)

3. A six-page, two-color folder on "How to earn more from your savings." (This was repetitive, with the exception of an example of investment growth and a history of the company.)

4. A small full-color leaflet offering two gifts.

5. A black and white leaflet about a bonus. (Again, repetitive.)

6. A red leaflet about a lump sum investment.

7. A small two-color folder on the plan outlined in the letter.

8. A two-page black and yellow memorandum. (Yet again repetitive, this time featuring duplicate information about the free gifts.)

One can only speculate as to why the mailing contained so much information. All the essentials were in the four-page letter, which should have been accompanied by a simple proposal form. Yet for all the flyers and photos, important facts about the company's history—and even essential facts about the investment plan—were vaguely presented or missing completely!

This was a mailing that may well have offered an excellent product, but that never fully explained the product. The copy simultaneously provided inadequate and superfluous information— and, as a result, severely diminished the offer's credibility. In this case, the mailing list may well have been excellent.

You must remember, though, that everything starts with the offer. It seems likely, then, that this offer served only to subsidize the postal service. The quality and appropriateness of a mailing must come first.

A GOOD MAILING PIECE

The second secret of success demands careful thought and precise planning. In succeeding chapters a variety of elements of a direct mailing are discussed: sales letters, one-piece mailers, envelopes, insertions, gimmicks and catalogues. The choices are so numerous that it is easy to be dazzled by the cleverness of some of the options.

Your choice lies largely in your understanding of the psychology of your recipient. Should it be a big four-color fold-out piece, or a simple sales letter? And how should it be packaged—what sort of envelope should you use? The basic principles to apply include the following, but your kind of business may suggest others.

Acceptability

What sort of mailing is most likely to be well received? Remember, receiving mail is often a pleasure. Don't abuse (as the junk mailers do) this initial advantage that direct mail has over any other advertising medium.

For instance, if you are planning a vacation and have applied for a brochure, the fun of planning a trip is enhanced when the printed envelope finally arrives. Even in an office setting this anticipation can be a factor (when the secretary sees that the envelope contains something for which the boss is waiting, for example).

But even if the mailing is unsolicited, it can be welcomed if it promises something interesting and useful. Remember Dr. Johnson's observation that advertising is all promise, great promise.

Relevance

Is the mailing relevant to the needs of the potential customer? This may depend on the selectivity of the mailing list—but even then, is the offer relevant to the chosen recipients? The question needs to be examined fully. When an insurance company mails to newlyweds, or to people recently promoted, the offer can be very relevant. The same can apply if a local store mails to all the residents of a new housing development. In all cases, the offer must be designed to suit the needs of the targeted consumer.

Credibility

Is the offer convincing? This element can cover either the benefits of the offer, your ability to give satisfaction, or both. Remember, although you may have been in business a long time, there are people who have never heard of you. It is easy to have a good mirror image of yourself—but the perceived image held by outsiders can be very different!

Therefore, it is important that the mailing establishes a clear corporate image. Make it clear who you are, what you do, how reliable you are, and so on. This may be done by explaining your history, quoting genuine testimonials, giving facts and figures where appropriate, and offering applicable guarantees or promises of replacements or refunds. Some mail order traders invite customers to visit showrooms.

The corporate image can be created by the kinds of merchandise or services you offer, or by the reputation you have built up over the years, or by the style of your mailing.

The style of your mailing is vital; it determines your corporate image. Does the mailing suggest that you are reputable and enterprising, or that you are too pushy?

The credibility factor is often ignored in the craze for cleverness. Direct response marketing has certainly grown, but it is full of cowboys who are destroying its credibility by overusing direct marketing sales gimmicks. The trouble with some of these techniques is that they have lost originality. Their novelty has waned, and as a result they have become ineffective. You can judge for yourself by what arrives in your own mail.

It is often argued, though, that new uses of old ideas may appeal to people in lower social stratas likely to be persuaded by these methods. It is still true that the most successful word in advertising is "free," but this word should be used legitimately. The magic appeal of such offers can be abused. If the "free" approach is applied to more serious or costly goods and services, then the risk of overkill destroys the offer's credibility.

For example, what is one to make of the following, adapted from a recent mailing?

Dear Mrs. . . .

IMPORTANT—IMMEDIATE RESPONSE REQUIRED

I am delighted to tell you that you have been selected to receive one of several valuable awards listed below:

CATEGORY A	CATEGORY B
Microwave Oven	Clock Radio
35 mm Camera	3 Piece Luggage
$150 Cash	14" Color TV

CATEGORY C
Video Recorder
$300 Cash
Home Burglar Alarm

Your award is determined by the code shown above and will be issued to you at our Award Center by matching the above number against our master list.

TO FIND OUT WHICH AWARD CATEGORY YOU ARE SELECTED TO RECEIVE call me TODAY at 508/555-8020 between 9:00 a.m. and 7:00 p.m. (Monday through Saturday) and I will also make an appointment for you to tour our Award Center and claim your award.

CALL US BETWEEN 9:00 A.M. AND 7:00 P.M. TODAY AT 508/555-8020 AND ASK FOR LISA. FIND OUT WHICH AWARD CATEGORY YOU ARE TO RECEIVE.

Call us now. Your award is awaiting your collection.

Yours sincerely,

Nancy Colvin
Award Liaison Manager

The way the letter was addressed reveals that "you have been selected" probably means something along the lines of "as one of the millions registered in the Publishers Clearinghouse Sweepstakes." Nowhere in the letter does it say what is being sold. It is only when one reads the information on the back that one finds out about a time-sharing promotion—and learns that participation is dependent on certain employment, income and marital conditions. The implication is that the recipient is guaranteed one of the nine awards. Is this too good to be true? Even if the reader manages to wade through the fine print on the back, will the skepticism subside long enough for him to make a phone call? The offer's credibility is stretched beyond belief.

Another company followed a variation on the same familiar routine by sending an advance letter warning recipients of their impending good fortune—a gimmick that has also lost its freshness. As always, the recipients of the offer are addressed as the chosen few. As one advance letter heralded: "I am very pleased to inform you that you are among those selected. . . ." One can imagine the labels pouring out of the computer printer. The main text of the mailing, the usual lie, went on:

    Before too long an envelope from
    ABC Alliance—clearly marked 'L38,750
    Special Invitation Prize Drawing—228
    Cash Prizes must be won!'—should ar-
    rive at your address.

As it happened, another envelope from the same company arrived on the same day. Pure luck determined which envelope got opened first. Adding insult to injury, more "altruistic" bureaucratese formed a P.S. to the advance letter:

    On behalf of all my colleagues at
    ABC Alliance, I recommend that you
    act promptly to take full advantage
    of all the opportunities it brings
    you.

What's more, I determined later that the mailing list itself had been completely mistargeted!

The two-page sales letter used for the second mailing, which coincided with the advance letter, was poorly written. It did not mention a prize drawing, but offered a choice of four free gifts. It was very confusing, and had nothing to do with selling the product. There was also the inevitable sampling of colored paper in various shapes and sizes.

Both letters were signed by the same manager, but one was addressed to the husband and one to the wife! This double mistake did nothing to reinforce what little credibility remained. The whole package was another appalling example of junk mail.

You may have realized by now that the company was conducting two entirely different direct response marketing schemes—each having free gift incentives. They were released simultaneously, either to the same or different mailing lists!

Unfortunately, you are at the mercy of the big spenders in direct mail marketing. They are capable of alienating your market by producing a high volume of junk mail. So study what you yourself receive, analyze it and learn from it.

A GOOD MAILING LIST

A good offer and a good mailing will fail or succeed according to the quality of the mailing list. This can be the most critical and difficult aspect of direct mail marketing.

The great advantage of direct mail is its ability to select prospects, and to appeal to them directly at their addresses. This compares favorably with the more hit-or-miss broadcast effect of the mass media. Ideally, that should mean that it is more economic and effective to work in direct mail than in print ads, radio, or TV.

Unfortunately, the very strengths of direct mail can be weakened if there are faults in the mailing system. The third secret of success lies in how efficiently you conduct your mailing. This will be dealt with more thoroughly in a separate chapter, but we will consider here the hazards associated with your mailing lists.

If you use directories or membership rosters as sources, your lists are bound to be slightly out of date; addresses are constantly changing. In addition, professional people often belong to more than one society or institute, and it may be difficult to avoid repeat mailings.

It may not be easy to de-duplicate computerized lists because a search may not locate variations in names. This problem is intensified when wrong spellings have been keyed in originally. When numerous errors occur (as with a name like mine!) it may be impossible to locate duplications, and multiple mailings will occur. Irritated recipients may complain—and find that their complaints have been ignored because the errors are repeated in the future. People are very vain about the correct spelling of their names. To maintain good relations, it pays to try to make corrections. However, this may not be possible if you are using someone else's database or list, and have no direct access to it.

One way to keep lists current is to send postcards to past recipients asking whether they still wish to be mailed. Lists based on coupon responses can accumulate beyond control. Such postcard checks are made by many firms in numerous settings, markets, and countries. The technique can help you avoid mailing expensive catalogues to people no longer interested, alive, or still living at the same address.

Consider your own experiences. Like most of us, you've probably discovered that when you move into a new residence, you're likely to receive mail—sometimes for years!—addressed to former occupants. It should come as no surprise, then, that the "shelf life" of most mailing lists is rarely more than six months.

When using list brokers or databases it is worth asking about the age of their lists, or how well they're updated. People are often very lax about reporting changes of addresses, and in your case there's often no reason why they should inform you. Lists also become out of date because people die, go abroad, change jobs or marry and change their names. The currency of a list is vitally important. Some waste is inevitable, but it can be minimized.

Frequency of mailings

The right frequency of mailings is a key issue, and represents a decision you should make right from the start. Some offers can be made only once; others should be followed up; periodic reminders may be desirable in some settings. You may make sequential mailings of different offers.

Limited time offers, follow-ups, reminders and regular mailings are strategies you must adopt as appropriate to your business. Regular mailings produce a sense of credibility; they establish your business as a permanent, reliable entity. Only you can prevent people from forgetting you. Repetition—intelligently used—is one of the most important tools available to advertisers.

Repetition does have its limits. One engineering company bored its trade customers by sending out a tedious monthly sales letter that amounted to little more than a waste of postage. If it is necessary to mail frequently, then be sure that each mailing contains an interesting and valuable offer. It helps if the recipient enjoys and benefits from your mailings. For example, a member of a book or record club will probably welcome the quarterly magazine containing new titles.

If a series is used, each succeeding letter should avoid making recipients feel they have been impolite in not responding to the previous one. It can present a new angle on the same subject. A series from a dry cleaner can be topical about the items that should be cleaned each month; a department store can offer topical or seasonal goods in a series of mailings. Series should be sent at reasonable intervals, such as monthly or quarterly.

Reminders are not always the same as series. It has been found that identical repeat mailings can be successful with the words "reminder" overprinted on the envelope or letter. This may seem a lazy sort of reminder, but there are always people who for one reason or another either misplaced or never saw the original mailing.

Reminders can also be made to follow up either inquiries or regular customers when the subject is topical. Examples might include automobile or household insurance and annual equipment servicing.

It is important to make sure that reminders have not been sent to people who have already responded and made purchases as this can irritate them. Obviously, this error can distort a mailing's perceived effectiveness (and irritate customers).

Follow-ups are often worth the trouble, provided they are tactful and supplement the sales offer with additional information or a new attraction. Take caution, however, not to fall into the trap of encouraging people to expect that there will be a worthwhile price reduction if only they wait long enough. This ploy of offering a set of reducing prices with succeeding follow-ups is used a great deal by correspondence schools; students seem to have learned to wait for the final "final" offer.

The failure to follow up can sacrifice business. If you are using your own database, it is easy to get the computer to run a batch of labels identified by inquiries made over a certain period of time. This can be done on virtually any self-respecting database software.

In-house or mailing house?

Should you run your own direct response unit, or should you pay for the services of a mailing house? Much will depend on the size of your operation, which may or may not warrant the expenditure on equipment. You should also take into consideration whether you have your own database of customers and inquiries.

There are other questions to ask, as well. Do you need outside advice, creative services, equipment, access to lists?

There are both large and small firms that do it themselves, but there are also many specialized direct mail houses that service clients of all sizes. In between are owners of databases and list brokers, two groups we'll examine more closely later in the book. Here, let us consider the pros and cons of the in-house unit.

Advantages of an in-house direct response unit

1. You have complete and instant control over the whole operation. This includes the purchasing of merchandise, creation of pieces, compilation of the mailing list, mailings, and recording of inquiries/sales.

2. You can produce your own mailing lists more critically and selectively, and with less risk of duplication or error.

3. You can use a personal computer to record the history of an inquiry, follow-up, or sale, or whatever sequence of information you wish to store. This can be used for future mailings.

4. You have absolute control over the timing of mailings. This may be critical with urgent or dated offers for which there is a need to move stock quickly. You may have to solve a cash flow problem in a hurry, or you may want to clear stock which is the end of a line, has suffered a price change, or has become obsolete.

5. You may want to make exclusive offers to specialized mailing lists.

6. You may also want to make your own follow-ups to inquiries that have not converted to sales, or customers who are late in payment.

In other words, with your own unit you have better control, you can be more flexible, and you can introduce various submailings.

Disadvantages of an in-house direct response unit

1. You must be creative, and be able to write sales letters or other mailing pieces. (Of course, you can use freelance services.)

2. You must be able to prepare material for print, and work with printers. This will involve layouts and artwork, and the preparation of typographical instructions.

3. You must be able to buy material for letterheads, artwork, photography and envelopes, and must be familiar with the suppliers of these items.

4. You must understand postal regulations and be able to work with your local post office.

5. You may need to buy equipment to reproduce, fold, insert and stuff mailings (although this will depend on the volume of work).

The Direct Mail House

1. The direct mail house is set up to handle everything creative and physical related to your mailing. This includes writers, artists, buyers and equipment.

2. It can offer professional advice on how to set up a direct marketing plan for your business.

3. In addition, the direct mail house has a pool of experience gained from handling campaigns for a variety of other clients.

4. If you are not planning to make large or frequent mailings, you can share creative and mechanical facilities that are too expensive for full time use.

5. The direct mail house will be familiar with sources of material to use in mailings (including envelope makers and printers), or suppliers of gifts and incentives.

Checklist for choosing a mailing house

1. Is the staff familiar with your kind of work? Pay a visit and find out.

2. What equipment do they have for reproducing, addressing, folding, filling, sealing, sorting and stuffing envelopes?

3. What are their relations with postal and other delivery services? Can they organize prompt, correctly timed, economical mailings?

4. Do they offer fulfillment services, or are they associated with a fulfillment house? (This would relate to the handling of coupons, sales promotion offers or orders.)

5. Do they offer 24-hour service?

6. Who are their envelope suppliers/printers? What variety of envelopes or overprinted designs do they offer? Do they offer shrink-wrapping, which you may need when mailing a catalogue or display pack?

7. Is their location convenient for you? (You may prepare or have produced mailings independently and only require mailing facilities.)

8. What are their list facilities? Do they work with list brokers or databases? Use geographic-demographic systems?

9. What creative services do they offer? Do they have their own writers, photographers and studio, or do they use freelancers and outside services?

10. Do they offer an advisory service? Will they plan campaigns for you?

11. What have they done for other clients? It will be worth studying examples of past work.

12. Do they service any of your competitors? In this highly competitive business, confidentiality may be necessary for security reasons.

13. Have they won any relevant awards, such as those from the American Direct Marketing Association?

14. What are their charges? These should be quoted for every operation.

The names and address of mailing houses will be found in such magazines as *Advertising Age*, *Direct Marketing*, and *Marketing News*.

Chapter Three

How to Write Sales Letters

Sales letters!

Receivers of direct mail often feel they are pestered with a flood of questions and propositions.

Writing sales letters is one of the most highly skilled forms of copywriting. A sales letter is not just a business letter. It is an advertisement.

Look more carefully at all those sales letters you receive— before you throw them away. *Why* do you throw them away? Because they are tedious, irrelevant, or both! Why are they tedious?

Length

Sales letter writers often suffer from verbosity. Perhaps they are written by sales managers who don't know when to stop dictating. Most sales letters are not composed creatively; these appeals should be boiled down until they convey the fullest message in the fewest words possible. Some letters extend over four or even six pages. One page is usually sufficient. Psychologically, the signature at the bottom of a one-page letter encourages you to read on. A continuation, on the other hand ("over, please" or "continued") is discouraging. Why design a letter that's a turn-off before it's read?

What was once called mail order is now called direct response *marketing*; maybe the marketing influence is not completely positive for direct mail. Marketing people tend to go in for a lot of words; they can convert a crisp, factual, newsy press release into pages of unpublishable verbiage.

It was way back in 1977 that David Ogilvy, in his keynote speech to the first Direct Marketing Day in London, said: "If anyone tells you that long letters don't sell, he doesn't know anything about direct mail."

At that time, it was possible to say a long sales letter could be justified, assuming that the offer was interesting and was directed at the right prospects. The whole direct marketing scene, however, has changed since Ogilvy's speech.

The sales letter must often compete for attention with its own enclosures. Broad-based lists, and the sheer quantity of mailings going out, have created competition for reading time. The day has passed when a consumer received an occasional direct mail piece and could spend time absorbing a long sales letter. Today, a short sales letter is more likely to be read. You can judge them for yourself if you are the receiver of a lot of direct mail. Which ones do you read: the short or the long sales letters? It makes the most sense to write copy that gets read.

Appearance

If one is writing a letter it should look like a letter, but many so-called sales letters resemble sales pamphlets. Some are more like newsletters. They are four- or six-page folders, printed on both sides. Why on both sides? You wouldn't type a letter on both sides of your letterhead, would you?

Small type

Some letters are miniaturized to get a lot of words on the sheet. Once again, they don't look like letters. They lack credibility.

Overpersonalization

Laser printing is very irritating when your name keeps appearing throughout the text of a letter. It is courteous to personalize the salutation. However, if this technique is overused, it will severely diminish the effectiveness of the sales letter.

Tedious, dull style

Letter writing is an art: a letter should be pleasant to read. This may be achieved by employing a strong, straightforward style and a varied vocabulary. A good test is to read a letter aloud.

Effective letters are developed by editing the draft and strengthening the overall delivery. You can paraphrase sentences. You can gain emphasis by starting key sentences with "and" or "but." You can use the one-word or one-sentence paragraph. You can use contractions ("wouldn't" instead of the more formal "would not"). In fact, the nearer a letter sounds like someone talking, the more natural, personal and friendly it becomes. A letter should read like a message from one person to another.

Some sales letters are pompous and pretentious. For example, the phrase "I am pleased to inform you" sounds as if your divorce has come through or someone has found your lost cat. A well written sales letter immediately wins the reader's interest and attention. The reader should be carried along by the pace of the letter. This does not mean that it has to be overexuberant, but the words must move along like the notes in a good tune. A variety of short and longer sentences can be used to develop a rhythm in the writing. A sales letter has to resemble a sports car, not a steamroller.

Short paragraphs—with indentations where white space leads the eye in again and again—can encourage the reader to read on.

That's another point. The block paragraphs of typical business letters do not encourage reading. You would not want to read a book or a newspaper that did not have indented paragraphs. So why not use them in a sales letter and make it more readable?

Overkill

Credibility is lost when a letter becomes too strident. The trouble with some sales letters is that they try too hard. You don't have to scream at people with underlining, bold type, capital letters or colors. These devices are fine in a press advertisement, a sales leaflet or a catalogue, but a letter should be a letter.

Charity appeals have to reach the reader on an emotional level. Consider the headline from this recent example:

<u>Will you give $25 this Christmas to help save a child's life?</u>

The first paragraph read:

Dear Friend:

<u>That may sound dramatic—but in this country, an average of three to four children a week die following abuse or neglect at the hands of parents or guardians.</u>

Let's analyze the letter further. The opening is a good, compelling opening paragraph, but the underlining was unnecessary. The rest of the letter ran to four pages on two sheets, using both sides of the sheet. Nice, crisp short paragraphs were used, but the letter was far too long. Interspersed on unnumbered pages 2 and 3 were photographs, which meant that the wording alongside had to be reduced to half column width. The flow of the reading was unsettled by this device.

On three pages, underlined words were also given a green "highlighter" effect. Four of these had big green crosses in the left margin. All this over-emphasis diminished interest, rather than attracting it. On page 4 there was a P.S. in typewriter script, followed by a P.P.S. in imitation handwriting, followed by a boxed message about reporting child abuse to a national hotline number. The writer simply could not let go.

Are postscripts necessary? There is a school of thought in direct mail that says they are, but the overall effect can be amateurish. In this instance, at any rate, there was, supplementing the letter with the two postscripts, a "brief note" from the director of the organization, two pages of reproduced press clippings, a donation form bearing yet another letter from a *third* person, and a reply envelope. As if that weren't enough, the mailing list was so ridden with duplicates that more than one person in the same household could expect to receive the same mailing.

And the reader's reaction to this hysteria? Probably something like, "If they can afford to waste money like this, they don't need anything from *me*!" That's unfortunate, because the letter describes a worthy cause—but potential donors are likely to resent being bludgeoned so hysterically and so wastefully. They didn't get my money, and I do respond to charity appeals. (The mailing did win an industry award, though!)

Another problem with charity appeals is that if you are a regular donor to charities, your name gets on lists that appear to be sold to other charities, and you are inundated with appeals week in and week out. The annoyance and waste factors must be massive, but such folly is only intensified when the letters are written and designed with such an air of desperation.

Insincerity and low credibility

Some sales letters are too effusive or pretentious. Even an overpersonalized salutation may be too chummy for a letter coming from a stranger. Another common example of insincerity is the "delight" or "pleasure" many writers express. Look at the following example:

```
Dear Homeowner:
I am delighted to welcome you to
the new, improved facilities and
wider range of products now available
at Maximum Output Building Supplies
in downtown Braintree.
```

"I am delighted" comes off as hackneyed, cloying, and unbelievable. Why are so many of today's letter-writers "pleased" and "delighted"? The misuse of these and similar phrases is easily the most amateur, boring, and stupid way to start a sales letter. What on earth does the writer really have to be pleased about? There would be more sense in saying that you will be delighted or pleased with something the letter has to offer, not the other way around!

THE FOUR-POINT FORMULA FOR GOOD SALES LETTERS

Having reviewed these seven stumbling blocks, we turn now to the positive aspects of a good sales letter. A strong format must be determined before you write anything—otherwise your letter will degenerate into a shapeless, turgid monstrosity pretending to be a sales letter (and, even worse, it won't generate sales).

Your letter must be planned; it must have a clear progression, dispensing information in a logical manner. You need a basic skeleton or synopsis—just as a professional writer does in preparing a book, play, poem, article, or even a news release.

Such a format imposes a discipline on the writer. Any number of structural decisions within the broad outline can work; you can decide which one suits you best. You may decide to blurt out your proposition right away, or you may want to introduce it in a more subtle manner. You might pose a number of questions, leading up to your solution as the proposition. However, here is a basic four-point formula you can follow that we will examine in detail.

1. Attention-getting opening paragraph.

2. Interesting proposition.

3. Convincing sales argument.

4. Action-prompting closing paragraph.

Attention-getting opening paragraph

The "grabber" opening paragraph is essential. But preceding the first paragraph, should there be a headline? In some cases, a headline definitely adds something. It may be used for emphasis, as an introduction, or a bold giveaway of the offer. ("YOU CAN SAVE AN ADDITIONAL 20% ON YOUR SUBSCRIPTION RENEWAL TO *NEWSWEEK*—BUT ONLY IF YOU ACT NOW!")

Of course, you may decide it's most appropriate to go straight into the letter. One way to win attention is to pose a question—but you have to be careful not to provoke a negative response which ends the reader's interest.

The opening paragraph is going to make or break the letter; you may find that you will have to rewrite it many times to get it right. (Keep in mind that the opening paragraph is usually the most difficult part of any literary exercise.)

You may find it is best to write the first paragraph last; after the main copy has been written, you will know what you want to lead into.

Interesting offer

After the opening paragraph should come the offer. We have already discussed the choice of offer and its relevance to those on your mailing list. The letter may run over a number of paragraphs; build this element up step by step to create interest and desire to buy.

Convincing sales argument

This may be implicit in the whole letter; on the other hand, you may need to lead up to convincing reasons why a purchase should be made. Some of the reasons may be:

1. The price—a special price, or a discount for quantity or an instant reply.

2. A limited time offer.

3. A gift offer.

4. Testimonials or proof of successful usage.

5. A guarantee or promise of a refund if not satisfied.

6. The opportunity to view the showroom.
   And so on.

Action-prompting closing paragraph

A direct mailing, which is static, must stimulate its readers to do something. What do you want them to do? Here are some suggestions:

1. Fill in the order form and make payment.

2. Phone in the order.

3. Invite a salesman to call.

4. Visit your showroom or shop.

5. Complete a reply card for samples.

Whatever the action, the last paragraph should serve as an initiator. Include all relevant contact information prominently, so as to make the next step easy for the reader. Telephone numbers with area codes or business reply envelopes, directions or maps, and/or clear instructions about payment, should be carefully thought out to overcome any type of sales resistance.

Put yourself in your reader's mind. Consider his or her role and its effect on decision-making. Like the first paragraph, this final solicitation is vital to the success of the mailing. Ideally, the preceding paragraphs should have prepared the reader for action.

Example of a sales letter

The following is an example of a letter that might be sent by a local newspaper advertisement manager to local businesspeople. In a fairly short space, it conveys pertinent and interesting facts in a compelling way—and leads convincingly to action on the reader's part.

```
Dear Mr. . . .

Do you know what 90,000 people do
on Fridays and over the weekend? They
don't all go fishing, or visit their
in-laws, or even play golf. They read
the Weekly Item. They could be your
customers.
Did you realize, with all the pub-
lications around these days, that so
many people still buy their local
newspaper? The fact is, our circula-
tion figures continue to rise, but
our advertising rates have stayed at
the same affordable level.
```

Daily newspapers are soon thrown away. The <u>Weekly Item</u> usually stays in people's homes until the next issue comes out. Household members refer to it throughout the week. Think how many times your advertisement can be seen by at least two if not three times the circulation figure! This means the <u>Item's</u> actual readership is more like a quarter of a million people.

If you want to use illustrations, picture quality is guaranteed by our computerized scanner. Full color displays are no problem. In addition, we have computerized typesetting equipment that offers 50 different typefaces, so your copy can have character and originality.

Your advertisement must reach us no later than noon Monday to appear in the same week's issue. Our rate card is enclosed. You may reserve space by phone—or mail or fax your copy and specifications to this office. (Our fax line: 617/555-1212.)

If you would like to discuss the most profitable way to promote your business, feel free to call. Our representative for your area will be happy to set up an appointment.

Sincerely,

In the above example, the letter contains a number of options; the advantages of the service offered are concrete, yet the prospect is unlikely to feel pestered.

While charity appeals have a reputation for being either dreary or overpowering, the following letter, from an organization for the blind, is irresistible. At least, that was my response.

The Gift of Sight

Dear Mr. Jefkins,

May I share with you a visit I made recently to the village of Gorai, near Dhaka, in Bangladesh. There I met Abdul the local weaver, creating his intricately patterned cloth on his wooden loom. Later that day, I was introduced to Zarina, who was preparing the evening meal in her brightly decorated hut. Outside, Mohsena her ten-year-old daughter was learning to read, write and thread a needle.

Weeks before, <u>they were all blind</u> . . . but then one of our medical teams, led by Doctor Hussain, conducted an 'eye camp' in their village. People came from miles around; tents became improvised wards; the school classroom was converted into a temporary operating theatre; and volunteers served hundreds of rice meals a day.

Ten days later, with the bandages removed, they opened their eyes to the first shock of light. In all, seventy-three blind villagers had their sight restored at that 'eye camp'. It seems a miracle, yet the cost to this Society was just £15 to perform these three operations for Abdul, Zarina and Mohsena.

During the last year, our medical teams have restored sight to 214 033 blind men, women and children. Yet, for each person in that multitude, sight came as an individual miracle. It was made possible because someone like you cared that a fellow human being might otherwise remain needlessly blind. No gift could have been more precious—but there remains so much still to do.

At this moment, in the impoverished countries where we work, there are nearly <u>seven million curably blind people</u>. After thirty-seven years of experience, our medical teams have a skill which, given the money, could restore sight to thousands more people during the next few months.

Will you invest in that skill? Will you spare £15 to give three people the incomparable gift of sight?... £160 would save the sight of a whole village in <u>*your*</u> eye camp.

Your help is desperately needed, but time is not on our side. Your generosity today will give sight, hope and independence tomorrow to people who must otherwise remain blind.

Yours sincerely,
Alan W Johns

P.S. Please close your eyes for a moment, and imagine what it would be like never to see again. Your gift of £15 (the equivalent of £1.25p per month) will restore sight to three more people who are needlessly blind.

That is a gem of a letter. So interesting, sincere and compelling! No gimmicks. And the only enclosures were useful ones: a donation form and a reply-paid envelope.

Chapter Four

How to Compile and Ensure Good Mailing Lists

Today, there is no difficulty in finding or creating a good mailing list. The wealth of directories, list brokers and databases, and computers make it easy to assemble in-house databases.

The problem lies in knowing how to select and use lists effectively and economically. Why subsidize the Postal Service?

Actually, we should not be too unkind to the Postal Service. As you will find in different chapters of this book, while obviously seeking to promote its own business (which is fair enough) it does offer a remarkable range of services you can exploit to make your mailings more efficient.

Research

A wealth of Postal Service literature is available on all these services; contact your local office for more information.

I am a great believer in and a successful user of direct mail, but every week I seem to fill up endless garbage sacks with discarded mailings. Many are thrown away because the sales letters are too long-winded—some warn me well ahead of time with their printed envelopes not to open them in the first place. If I ever win anything as a contestant on a TV game show, I pray it's my own personal dumpster.

My name and address (in numerous formats and incorrect versions) is on a whole library of mailing lists and databases. My experience is common. Direct marketing is an excellent advertising medium that is being abused by carelessness and overkill.

To make your use of direct mail effective, you must select and control your mailing lists. It will save you a fortune—and will keep you from alienating your market. Learn to be a miser over your direct mail efforts; avoid blanket mailings. You'll stand out from others marketing the same product or service. (By way of example, let me point out that when I mail 4,000 pieces, some of my competitors send out 25,000. I am on their lists. I receive up to six of their mailing pieces. You might ask why they bother to mail to me!)

Virtually every organization has some kind of list of members, customers, or donors that can be useful to someone else. Membership lists of societies, the Yellow Pages, and electoral rolls are easily available. (Often, you can tell the origin of some lists by careful study of the way the address is composed.) "I've got him on my list!" is the common cry of direct mail. Not surprisingly, the sale of lists to list brokers, or the direct rental of one's list, is producing significant incomes for many organizations.

BUILDING YOUR OWN LIST

You may decide to build your own list. You can maintain it yourself, and supply it to a list manager or to a direct mail house, which can computerize it and use it for your mailings. If you build your own list, you need to decide how often it will be used. This depends on the nature and size of your business.

For instance, if you are mailing a prospectus or list of events (such as courses, concerts or plays) it may pay to produce a new list each time, using whatever resources are up to date. For more frequent mailings, you can have a live, cumulative list, updated regularly with deletions, additions and amendments.

It is a fatal mistake to rely on an ever-accumulating list that is only added to but never changed. Too many in-house lists continue to contain non-responsive, incorrect, and non-existent addresses. This is the lazy man's way to build a mailing list, but it is all too common.

People often call me asking to be placed on my mailing list; they are surprised when I tell them I do not keep one. That is not entirely true—my office is full of list sources, and some are computerized on a short-term basis. The type of list I use, however, is relevant to the mailing being assembled. This involves a considerable selection process, with the result that addressing, envelope, print, filling and postage costs are minimized. I spend the least, in other words, to get the most.

The problem with renting lists is that you may have no way to check how well they are maintained by the original compiler. Your own database lists are probably more accurate because there are computer facilities for maintaining them. Lists that reflect reader inquiries to advertisements are often out of date after six months; the recipients are never likely to notify changes in status, job or private addresses.

Here are some ways in-house lists (including databases) can be created. You may be able to use some of these selection criteria as they apply to your particular business.

Sources for in-house lists

Customers

These can be classified by:

1. Sex

2. Age

3. Job Title

4. Location

5. What they bought

6. Value of purchase

7. Method of payment:
   (a) Cash

   (b) Installments

   (c) Credit

   (d) Credit card

8. Frequency of purchases

9. Date of last purchase

10. Department/branch bought from

Of course, you can incorporate any other applicable classification—depending on whether you are a bookseller, printer, insurance broker, service engineer, department store manager, etc.

Most basic database software can be set up to file this information. The information can be called up and flagged as required for printing out labels and recording follow-up.

Directories and membership lists

Numerous trade directories are available, and you may be able to obtain the membership lists of many national and local societies. You can also consider sources such as the Yellow Pages and electoral rolls. It will pay to obtain this type of information each year.

But there is both an advantage and a disadvantage to this approach. Inevitably, the information in these books cannot be 100 percent up-to-date at the time of publication, and many changes of address will occur as the year progresses. Not many publishers issue quarterly updates, or have on-line current data, but some do offer update facilities. You may be able to correct such sources by watching out for changes of address announcements in the relevant trade press. This can entail a lot of work, however, and you may simply have to risk making some mistakes when using directories. If you are using directories, it is wise to discard old editions and invest in the latest, even if the price is steep. Of course, if you keep your eyes open, you may be surprised at how many up-to-date lists can be found in publications you may already have.

A warning: membership lists have the weakness that they do not include the deletions and additions that occur after publication.

Newspapers, magazines, trade and professional journals

Additions or amendments to your mailing list can be made by subscribing to the journals relevant to your market. The sections outlining recent promotions and hirings can be useful. Personal notices of engagements and marriages may also be another source. Marketing intelligence information (such as listings of new companies, tenders and contracts) is an excellent source for updating your mailing list. It may pay to visit a good library and see what journals you should consider subscribing to, or, in the case of "controlled circulation" publications, asking to receive for free.

Inquiries

Whether they're general inquiries by mail or telephone, or received in response to print advertising, customer queries can be incorporated into your mailing list. However, you must use discretion in evaluating their validity after a certain time.

You may decide to eliminate all those that have not been converted to the customer file after six months. This must be your decision, based on your type of business and the prospect in question. Students are unlikely to be useful after they have completed a course of instruction; gardeners may go on gardening all their lives. Similarly, you must also learn to sense once-only buyers: real estate agents sometimes make the mistake of mailing material to people long after they have probably bought a house and moved.

Warranty cards

If a person has purchased a household item and returned a warranty card, he or she is an excellent prospect to buy something else. This type of response is a very high quality source you can use to update your mailing list.

OTHER PEOPLE'S LISTS AND DATABASES

Many owners of lists are willing to rent them. This can be a good way to reach specialized groups of prospects you could not otherwise locate. Consider even unusual sources to target groups such as:

1. Buyers of women's fashions

2. Professional people

3. Correspondence school students

4. Academics

5. Caterers

6. Travel brochure applicants

7. Purchasers of security equipment

8. Visitors to trade exhibitions

9. Buyers of furniture covers

Lists can be managed by companies with computer facilities for holding, updating and maintaining lists supplied by direct marketing clients. List brokers offer a wide variety of lists for rental to clients. See the Appendix for more information.

Numerous databases or megalists are available to direct marketers; some will be demographically oriented. These have been called the "next generation of mailing lists," and have evolved from the consumer lifestyle studies conducted by advertising chieftain Leo Burnett in the 1970's.

These "enhanced" lifestyle databases offer much more intimately defined lists than traditional databases. You can, for instance, rent lists selectable by:

1. Psychographic/family lifestyles

2. Credit card ownership

3. Business/personal travel details

4. Investment/insurance ownership

5. Health/fitness interest

6. Outdoor activity interests

7. Sporting interests

8. Social and charity interests

9. Collectors

10. Fine food and wine interest

11. Types of electrical goods owned

12. Demographics

13. Home ownership

14. Type and length of residence

15. Marital status

16. Exact age of all adults

17. Presence and ages of children or

18. Grandchildren

19. Income

20. Occupation

21. Working women

22. Types and numbers of cars

The purveyors of these lists point out that consumers they identify are highly responsive to direct mail since, when completing questionnaires identifying their characteristics and interests, they identified themselves as were mail responsive and asked to receive special offers or mail that matched their interests. To a considerable extent these lists can help you to avoid junk mail, and to minimize waste. See the Appendix for more information on list brokers.

List and database management firms can offer "merge/purge" services that combine lists while searching for duplications, inaccurate, incomplete or changed addresses. De-duplication procedures are also applied by checking zip codes—as well as data such as date of birth and telephone number. To do this, they use what is called a "tie-breaker" device.

Net names

Net names are effectively a discount system for volume users of third-party mailing lists.

List rental prices are generally non-negotiable, and as a user of lists, you will be quoted the same price even if you approach the list owner, the list manager or the broker about rental of a particular list.

However, if you intend to carry out a de-duplicaton exercise (merge/purge) prior to mailing, you may not physcially mail all the names supplied on a particular list. This is because the same individuals may appear either on your own list or on two or more of the lists you are renting. It is a waste of time and money to mail any individual more than once in a particular mailing.

History and experience have shown that after de-duplication, you are likely to use about 85 percent of the names supplied. This quantity will vary depending on the numbers you are mailing, the size of your own list, and the accuracy with which you are targeting the third-party mailing lists. However, the 85 percent figure has been identified as an industry norm. As a result, many list owners, managers and brokers will offer an "85 percent net names arrangement" on orders for list quantities of over 10,000 (or, in some cases, 20,000) names and addresses. This means that you pay full rental price for at least 85 percent of the names supplied. Typically, if you only mail 75 or 80 percent of the list, you will still be obliged to pay for 85 percent; if you mail 90 or 95 percent, you will be charged at full rental price for this percentage.

In addition, you will be required to cover the list owner's computer charges for the unused balance. These are known as "running" or "run-on" charges.

Some list sources may give more favorable net name deals on very large quantity orders from a particular list. In the business-to-business sector, net name arrrangements are less common, and tend to apply only to the very large mailers. In the international sector, net names are largely unknown.

Even if you have agreed to a net names percentage discount, you will generally be invoiced initially for 100 percent of the names supplied. This is later adjusted by means of a credit note once the computer department has undertaken the de-duplication work and has submitted proof of the final figures.

Examples of databases or megalists

Dun and Bradstreet has massive files of active businesses extracted from D&B's overall database of millions of American businesses. This source offers selection by standard industrial classification codes (SIC codes), size of company by turnover or employees, and location at start-up date; the listings feature named executives, as well. Dun and Bradstreet is committed to quality, and has taken the trouble to reduce "forwarding-order-expired" problems by pruning hundreds of thousands of out-of-date records. They guarantee a refund if a mailing using their database has more than a 3.5 percent "moved-away" rate. Their experience points to the danger of a database on which it may be easier to include than exclude an address. How old, how well maintained, is the database you propose using—including your own?

The variety and specificity of the lists available to you is truly staggering. One source I worked with offered a list of 380,000 people who had recently purchased or inquired about self-development and leisure courses. Demographically, the breakdown was as follows: aged 20-35, approximately 65 percent male, 35 percent female.

Another source offered a database of 250,000 contacts involved with the catering industry, including restaurants, hotels, pubs, canteens, fast food outlets and local caterers.

This should give you an idea of the breadth of the available ready-made specialized lists on computer databases that may be useful to you.

TARGETING

Targeting is the name of the game, although what can be classified as junk mail is still dependent on the recipient's reaction. Targeting is the means of cutting costs and maximizing response. It brings direct mail in line with traditional above-the-line media planning and buying.

You may or may not agree with this, but it has been proposed that one way to determine age group in a list consisting of names and addresses is the first name. These first names tend to belong to particular periods and are associated with factors like the popularity of film stars and pop singers.

Piggybacking

Another option that may be useful to you in both targeting and ensuring economy is what is variously known as piggybacking, bounceback, third-party mailing, or swap mailing. Your piece is inserted with someone else's mailing when the list is appropriately targeted. A typical example is the sort of insertion you often find with your monthly or quarterly bill. Alternatively, the insertion could be placed inside a package containing goods a customer has already ordered.

There are pros and cons to piggybacking. You will save on postage; the recipient has only one envelope to open. If your mailing is of interest to the recipient, that's all well and good. However, the enclosure can be an irritant if the recipient wants to read the bill and finds extraneous pieces of paper in the envelope. In the case of the parcel, the recipient will probably want to look at the goods and will not be deterred by irrelevant insertions. So much depends on the relevance of the insertion. If it adds something of interest and value to the original mailing, good. A buyer of records, cassettes or compact discs may be interested in associated equipment from another supplier.

The PRIZM System

One of the most exciting demographic research developments in the United States has been Claritas Corporation's PRIZM system. The acronym stands for Potential Rating Index Zip Markets, and is based on the idea that a group of consumers living within a given area will tend to share certain tastes and outlooks of interest to marketers. The principle, according to Claritas, is that "birds of a feather flock together"; in other words, that consumers can be targeted for marketing purposes by classifying them within one of 40 groups (with names such as Golden Ponds, Young Influentials, and Black Enterprise) and keying the groups with neighborhoods identified through the zip code system.

"Through a complex statistical analysis of its demographic characteristics and actual consumer behavior," Claritas explains, "every U.S. neighborhood, over 500,000 in all, is assigned to one of the 40 PRIZM clusters." Do the "birds" within the clusters behave similarly, as predicted? The results seem to back up Claritas' claims for this segmented approach. It turns out, for instance, that in areas where *The New Republic* is a popular subscription magazine, croissants are consistently more popular than white bread (see *The Clustering of America* by Michael J. Weiss, Perennial Library, 1988). Organizations conducting subscription mailing campaigns (such as Washington D.C.'s National Symphony Orchestra), magazines targeting mailings to attract new subscribers (such as *Time*, *Newsweek*, and *McCalls*), as well as many other users, have found the PRIZM system to be effective.

On the following pages is a breakdown of the forty PRIZM clusters. To which group or groups are you addressing your messages?

WHO IS YOUR CUSTOMER, ANYWAY?

Odds are, according to Claritas Corporation, that he or she fits into one of its forty PRIZM cluster groups. The categories are reproduced below in descending order of average household income.

(Cluster descriptions courtesy of, and reproduced with the permission of, Claritas Corporation.)

Blue Blood Estates

This cluster comprises America's wealthiest neighborhoods. The upper crust finds its roots in "old money" families of white-collar professionals who live in suburban homes. Twenty percent earn over $100,000 a year. The tastes and inclinations of this group often determine what is considered high status in the United States.

Money and Brains

This group is characterized by elegant apartments, ritzy condos and renovated townhouses that bed well educated, white-collar professionals in our nation's largest cities. These areas attract our country's affluent intellectuals in the fields of science, business, academia, and politics. They are conscious of their business and academic achievements and happy to be so; they often consume, as the saying goes, conspicuously.

Furs & Station Wagons

This group represents "new money" ensconced in metropolitan bedroom suburbs that require a significant commute to the city. Politically conservative, members of this cluster have "made it" and have every intention of passing affluence on to their children.

Urban Gold Coast

Urban Gold Coasters are housed in expensive high-rise developments. The majority are childless, white-collar renters. The cluster is most noticeable in the metropolitan New York City and Chicago areas.

Pools & Patios

Residents are members of older, upper-middle-class suburban communities. These empty-nesters are quite comfortable with two-career incomes. Their Sunday afternoons are often spent at barbeques and parties; their politics tend to be conservative.

Two More Rungs

This cluster encompasses a group of upper-middle-class communities whose residents have achieved significant educational and professional success. The groups (typically, grown children of European immigrants) are found primarily in and around major cities.

Young Influentials

Young Influentials are childless Yuppies who live in condos and apartment complexes on the outskirts of major cites. They tend to be fast trackers with a taste for whatever is "hot." They are among the most-sought consumers in the nation.

Young Suburbia

"Baby on Board!" Young Suburbia is where many white-collar baby-boomers go to nest, typically in suburbs surrounding major cites. Cluster members are predominantly white families with college educated spouses in white-collar jobs.

God's Country

America's most recent pioneers. These people simply grew tired of the cities; they are high-income ex-urban boomtown residents with predominatly white-collar jobs and college educations.

Blue-Chip Blues

This cluster contains the wealthiest blue-collar households. Here adults with high school educations earn between $25,000 and $50,000 annually. Married couples are the norm. Group members may indulge in snowmobiles, boats, or pools.

Bohemian Mix

These urban dwellers, who live in inner-city regions such as New York's Greenwich Village, are a mixture of never-married and divorced singles, as well as young turks and older professionals. The group encompasses a unique profile of high- and low-income residents. Members tend toward political liberalism.

Levittown, USA

Levittowners are aging post-World War II homeowners whose main priorty is to maintain the status quo. These empty-nesters have extra dollars to spend on gadgets. They tend to be fiscally conservative, but more traditionally liberal on issues of foreign affairs.

Gray Power

This cluster consists of upper-middle-class communities with older residents. They are primarily concentrated in the Sunbelt region; their communities are self-contained. Residents no longer worry about urban blight, rush hour traffic, crime, or other problems of the big cities.

Black Enterprise

Residents are predominantly members of black middle- and upper-middle-class inner-city communities. They are well-educated; the guiding value in the cluster is that hard work and discipline lead to color-blind success.

New Beginnings

Middle-class city neighborhood residents, these single and divorced apartment dwellers tend to have some college education. Many of their neighborhoods are located in Sunbelt cities that are experiencing growth; many Northeasterners have moved here to seek new job opportunities.

Blue Collar Nursery

This group contains America's starter families who are located on the fringes of midwestern towns. The head of the household is usually a skilled laborer; a homemaker here may also be a secretary or nurse.

New Homesteaders

New Homesteaders moved out of the crowded cites to live life at a less hectic pace. They are predominantly white middle-class families with some college education, holding blue- or white-collar jobs.

New Melting Pot

This is the modern version of America's much-romanticized immigrant past. The latest wave of immigrants is composed primarily of Hispanics, Asians and Middle Easterners. This cluster should not be pigeonholed as being poor or uneducated; more than one-third have college degrees and home values of more than $100,000.

Towns & Gowns

These are America's college towns, with economies fueled by the local university. The populace is typically composed of two distinct groups: locals and students. The locals predominate, by an average three-to-one margin. High percentages of well-educated 18- to 24-year-olds live side-by-side with older blue-collar workers of more modest means.

Rank & File

The Rank & File cluster is composed of older, blue-collar industrial suburbs. These neighborhoods grew around "smokestack" industries. Residents are likely to have strong ties to organized labor; over 81 percent work in durable goods manufacturing jobs.

Middle America

These are quiet, midscale neighborhoods characterized by unpretentious homes, family-owned businesses and a widespread enthusiasm for local sports. As the name implies, Middle America residents reflect national norms on a number of fronts, including age and family size.

Old Yankee Rows

This cluster encompasses a mixture of blue- and white-collar old ethnics who make their homes in working class row district houses. The neighborhoods are located mostly in and around cities in the Northeast, and residents tend to be affliated with some type of union.

Coalburg & Corntown

These are small towns based on light industry and farming located in the Midwest. Most residents are high-school educated and earn under $35,000 a year.

Shotguns & Pickups

Residents of isolated lower-middle-class communities in mountainous rural areas make up these neighborhoods. The cluster is composed primarily of white families; high-school educations are the norm, as are blue-collar or farm jobs.

Golden Ponds

Golden Ponds are rustic cottage communities located near the coasts or along mountain lakes and streams. Residents are a mixture of outdoor enthusiasts, retirees, and townsfolk.

Agri-Business

Agri-Business centers are composed of small towns surrounded by large-scale farms and ranches located in America's plain or mountain states. These mid-level farm and ranching communities are composed primarily of white families in single-unit housing.

Emergent Minorities

These urban areas are predominantly black neighborhoods a step above the bottom-tier Public Assistance ghettos. Emergent Minorities residents work to move up the social scale and escape the poverty of the inner city. Unemployment is high; for many residents, high school diplomas are the highest level of education.

Single City Blues

Residents of these downscale, urban, singles districts may be said to live in a low-rent version of Bohemian Mix. They are racially mixed singles who live in multi-unit housing around major universities.

Mines & Mills

Residents of these struggling steel and mining communities are getting scarce. Many of these towns, concentrated between the Northeast and Lake Michigan, are in a period of steep decline.

Back-Country Folks

These people live in remote, downscale farm towns. Residents are predominantly white families that farm or hold blue-collar jobs.

Norma Rae-Ville

Lower-middle-class mill towns and industrial suburbs located in the south are home to members of this racially mixed cluster group. Most of the workers in these towns are not well educated and are accustomed to low-paying manual labor jobs.

Smalltown Downtown

These are inner-city districts of smaller industrial cities; the lower-middle-class residents are hangers-on who ignored or could not join the exodus to the suburbs.

Grain Belt

Those who still live in these low-population agricultural communities have been hit hard by the economic reverses in the farm economy of the mid-to-late 80s. Income levels are noticeably lower than those of Agri-Business residents.

Heavy Industry

Northeastern cities are the prime (but not sole) region for this cluster group, consisting of those living in urban manufacturing sectors now in a state of decline. Residents are typically non-white, older, and poor.

Share Croppers

This cluster is located primarily in small Southern towns where farming and light industry predominate. Racially mixed communities with grade-school educations are the norm.

Downtown Dixie Style

These are aging, predominantly black neighborhoods in Southern cites. The population is poorly educated and mostly lower-class. Some younger whites have been known to take advantage of comparatively low housing costs and move here.

Hispanic Mix

This cluster group comprises America's Hispanic barrios. The neighborhoods are made up of large families near the bottom of the income scale housed in older multi-unit dwellings.

Tobacco Roads

Tobacco Roads are racially diverse farming communities located in the South; cluster group members live in single-unit farmsteads, and are employed in blue-collar or farm jobs. They tend to have grade-school educations.

Hard Scrabble

These are the country's poorest rural settlements. Residents live in isolated communities, typically in single family dwelling units. They barely eke out a living from farm or blue-collar occupations.

Public Assistance

This group lives in America's inner city ghettos. Many are on welfare. The challenges of drug abuse, severe urban decay, and crime make daily life here difficult, exhausting, and dispiriting. Opportunities are few, and income levels rank at or near the nation's lowest for most residents.

The PRIZM system has applications in three main areas: explaining differences in behavior among consumers; targeting media campaigns; and locating prospects. It may not be appropriate (or cost effective) for your mail order business, but the underlying principles—and the descriptions of the target groups—merit a close look from anyone interested in marketing over the next decade. For more information on this increasingly influential approach to identifying and targeting consumers, you can contact Claritas Corporation at 201 North Union Street, Alexandria, Virginia 22314. The phone number is (703)683-8300.

Chapter Five

Insertions

What should comprise a complete mailing?

Other chapters discuss individual items from sales letters to gimmicks, and one chapter is devoted to the one-piece mailer. In this short chapter, let us consider what may be included in a mailing—and why.

If several enclosures are necessary, the order in which they should be taken out of the envelope—even the side that's placed up—can be important. This tactic is not always observed, and as a result, upon opening the envelope the recipient often does not know what to read first. Plan out exactly how you would like the recipient to review the information you present. This is elementary advice—but why is it so rarely observed?

1. Is a sales letter sufficient? Do you really need inserts?

2. What is the minimum necessary content of your mailing? An essential combination might be a sales letter, order form and reply envelope.

3. Will the cost of insertions really be justified by either response or increased response (note that the two are different)? Are you trying too hard?

4. Will the weight of insertions increase your postal costs—and is this extra cost likely to be justified by better results?

5. Will insertions increase the envelope size, and will that extra cost be justified by results? As we shall see, envelope size has a psychological effect on which envelopes to open first.

6. What does the recipient need to find in the envelope in order to be sufficiently interested and convinced to take positive action?

7. Are your proposed insertions likely to be helpful and action-provoking—or confusing, discouraging and extravagant? To help you to decide, collect the mailings you receive yourself and judge your own reactions. If you want a second or third opinion, ask your spouse or secretary to do the same.

8. Is the bulk of the envelope likely to create a bad impression before the envelope is opened? Will you merely tempt people to say "It's only junk mail"?

9. Do you need a sales letter at all? Is a folder, brochure or catalogue sufficient by itself? Is a one-piece mailer adequate?

The art of good advertising is simplicity. Do your insertions comply with this basic rule? If you have doubts on this score, consider some of the reasons why simplicity is so important.

Your mailing is probably unsolicited and unexpected. It may benefit from the element of surprise and be welcomed, but this is unlikely. Mail to commercial addresses can add to the burden of correspondence. A secretary will cull sales-oriented mail from apparently "real" business correspondence. She may even open large envelopes last! Mail to domestic addresses may have to compete with other direct mailings. If your piece is the only mail received, this could be disappointing, since it is not personal mail.

When planning a mailing, try to minimize sales resistance by anticipating the likely reaction when your piece is received. A standard envelope may be better received than something larger. A window envelope may save double addressing, but it suggests business correspondence rather than a private letter, and probably will be taken for a bill.

Your objective is to get the most business at the least cost. Designers may well concentrate on being creative rather than on necessity, utility and economy. When giving an order to a direct mail house or studio, you must first determine what you want. Costs will be discussed more fully later in the book.

This brings us right back to your budget: how much do you plan to pay per mailing? Money can quickly vanish on elaborate mailings that may be no more effective than something simpler. Complicated mailings can deter response, however ingenious you may think (or be told) they are.

It is necessary for the recipient to understand your offer as quickly as possible. Interest is easily lost or diverted, so it pays to get to the point as soon as you can.

Don't frustrate understanding and interest with a mailing that's too "busy."

The sincerity of your offer can be enhanced by its simplicity of attack. This goodwill element can be overshadowed by elaborate mailings. People are not going to sit down and meticulously study every word and every item if you overwhelm them with long letters and too many enclosures.

Response is more easily won if you make it easy to decide and act. But there is always the recipient's temptation to put it aside and deal with it "when there's more time" (which may be never). The problem with most printed advertising is that it is static and silent. Somehow you must prod the recipient into taking action.

Another way to promote action is curiosity. Does your mailer provoke a need to find out more? Too-clever "teaser" tactics can be irritating, but if you use some device—like posing an unusual question in the first paragraph of the sales letter—you can overcome the static nature of the medium. Put a smirk on the face of the reader, make him raise his eyebrows or nod his head. Provoke physical response if you can.

As you will see in the next chapter, the one-piece
mailer has the merit of simplicity, and it can create
curiosity and move the recipient to take action.

Chapter Six

One-piece Mailers

Although the issues of what to put in the mailers and how to keep down costs are addressed elsewhere in this book, we should note that the single-piece, complete-in-itself mailing has very definite advantages. That has been my experience, at any rate.

It may, of course, be essential to have more than one item. A sales letter may be necessary to introduce a catalogue or to highlight certain new items in it. It all depends on your business. You must decide what is most likely to work best for you. In my business, I prefer the one-piece mailer. Everything the prospects want to know is there on one piece of paper; the order form can be detached from the mailer. Some people photocopy the order form and retain the mailer intact.

A one-piece mailer says and does everything within a single piece of print. The order form can even be detached and folded to form a business reply item, thus saving a reply envelope. The mailer can be a folder or a booklet, but one large sheet of paper folding down like a map has the following special merits.

1. The broadsheet can fold down to a convenient envelope size. But watch the size of the sheet and weight of the paper; thick, hard-to-fold stocks will make the envelope-stuffing stage needlessly difficult. You may have to use a slightly less bulky stock, or have six rather than eight panels. If you are mailing overseas, it will be economical to keep the total weight of the mailer and envelope modest. Make tests; sample papers and envelopes before ordering your piece.

2. The whole mailing is compact and attractive to the recipient. Everything he wants to know is there where he wants it; he can put it in his inside pocket. The convenience factor is very strong.

3. The piece encourages immediate attention because of the size of envelope. There is a curious psychology about envelopes, which is worth repeating here. If you open your own mail, which envelopes do you select first? Most people open the smaller business size envelopes first because they expect them to be most important. Maybe they contain checks! Window envelopes, though, especially the smaller ones, usually contain bills. Large envelopes are less likely to contain business letters and are often left to last. The one-piece mailer in a standard business-size envelope asks to be opened along with the most important mail.

4. Especially if the front panel is intriguing, curiosity will encourage your prospect to unfold the mailer to see what's inside. If you can induce curiosity, you will have captured the reader's attention. And if your information is well arranged, you will lead the recipient on and on through your sales message. Remember, creating action on the part of the reader is your main goal! He or she should be eager to absorb what you have to say. In the end, the reader can have a complete spread of information that is not confined to separate panels but, like a map, allows the observer to "travel" a certain predesigned landscape in his imagination.

5. Envelope stuffing of single-piece mailings is easy. (But insert the piece so that when it is taken out, the most important panel is visible first.)

Points to consider

There are a few special points to remember about one-piece mailers:

1. The whole sheet should be designed so that the folds (and the unfolding) follow a coherent sequence. It shouldn't be necessary to have to turn the sheet upside down. This applies to the layout of both sides.

2. The front panel—the part that is immediately visible—should not just be a title. It should be either a digest of the contents or some device that will attract attention and urge the recipient to unfold the mailer. One device is to use a cut-out to reveal part of a picture inside.

3. Your firm's address and telephone number should be clearly displayed, easily found, and repeated if necessary. Don't make the mistake of putting it on the order form only. If this is detached and mailed, the customer is left with no contact information should this be needed later on.

4. The order form should be positioned where it is easiest to cut out, for instance, in a position with two outside edges. It may help to print a dotted line around the two inside edges of the order form. Otherwise people may be inclined to return the whole mailer, which can be a nuisance to you.

5. When planning the layout of the mailer, think how it can be most convenient, both to the recipient and to you. Make it easy for the customer to find out what he needs to know. For instance, if there are several items on the order form, then provide a small box by each item (and maybe the price). These boxes can be checked off to show exactly which item or choice is required.

If the customer has a choice of colors, it is a good idea to ask for a second choice. Prices should state whether they include shipping and handling, or whether this charge has to be added. Don't assume that the customer will know that the postage is included in your price.

It may be a psychological mistake to make a price look cheaper by failing to include such items; people may resent the hidden extras. If your mailing is to both home and overseas prospects, make sure you have separate prices such as airmail prices. Postage abroad can be more expensive than you think.

Again, with overseas mailings insist on payment with the order, preferably in U.S. dollars to avoid currency charges. Unless you have some special agency arrangement, never give credit to anyone overseas, for you have no means of recovering foreign debts. Our banks have discovered that!

What the customer needs to know is important. It is easy for you to ask for what you need to process the order. But is the product information so explicit that the reader cannot be puzzled? Become annoyed? Make a mistake? An uncertain customer is a lost one.

In most cases the prospect will not take the trouble to write or phone to ask what you haven't told him. It is up to you to think of every possible reason why your prospect may hesitate to order, and to have an answer. Have you left anything out?

What must you tell him to convince him and so secure his order? Does he need to know how long it will take to deliver the goods? Is there immediate delivery on receipt of checks? Or do you wait for a check to be accepted by the bank? Must the order be prepaid, or will you invoice? Depending on your clientele, "Send no money now" may be a good inducement, or it could create bad debts! To whom should the customer make out the check? Do you advise registered mail for payments, especially from overseas? Do you accept only U.S. dollars from abroad? Do you accept credit cards? Is your offer good for a limited time only? Do you offer goods "on approval," allowing return of those items that do not meet with a customer's satisfaction, and billing only for what is kept? There are a lot of questions, but getting paid or making it easy to pay are important, however you look at it.

All such details should be made crystal clear. You do not want to get involved in time-consuming correspondence or telephone calls. Nor do you want to get bogged down in debt collecting. People who owe you money for an extended period generally come to hate you. You must not discourage orders simply because you have failed to put yourself in your prospect's shoes. The customer is not an idiot: but he won't know what to do unless you tell him.

The wording needs to be fully detailed and free of ambiguity. Use short words, short sentences, short paragraphs. Set your material out with subheadings and good use of white space so that there is not a formidable amount of gray reading matter. Introduce contrast by employing subheadings in a bold or different typeface. Don't frighten people by making the mailer look like a boring mass of words.

People do want to know everything that will interest them and give them confidence in making a purchase, but people can be quite lazy about reading. A lot of words may be necessary, but you must not make them look like a lot!

If prospects don't want to read, how can you overcome this problem? Photographs, sketches, cartoons and diagrams can help. It is true that a picture is worth considerably more than a thousand words, as any Sharper Image catalogue will demonstrate. There's no point in saying a bomber jacket makes a distinctive fashion statement unless people can see its sleek leather and appealing cut. There really are people who don't know what a bomber jacket looks like or, if they do, what it is called. Remember this when describing goods. Sometimes there are trade names and popular names. Think how many articles of clothing are just called "jackets." Do you think a photograph of the particular jacket you'd like to sell for $75 would help your cause?

A picture of a person can communicate a message more effectively or convincingly than mere words. This may be a picture of you, or of a model using your product, or a drawing of a typical user. You don't have to use something ridiculous like a bikini-clad blonde wearing high-heel shoes and driving a power mower (it's been done), but people often identify with pictures. A stout, middle-aged man may buy a pair of slacks because an attractive, athletic-looking young man is wearing them. He wants to look like that dashing young man. He wants to believe he still is a dashing young man.

A very simple way to emphasize or pinpoint items is to use a second color for subheadings, or to set black type on a colored panel. But don't use too hard a background color; it can kill the copy it's supposed to enhance. Also, be careful of reversing type to read white on a color. This is dangerous unless the wording is very large for the sake of good contrast; 50 percent of the legibility can be lost by reversing small type.

You may not be a designer or a copywriter, and you may have to rely on outsiders for creativity, but only you can put yourself in the place of your customer. That's why it is so important to be a good communicator. Ask yourself: what does your prospect need to know? What do you need to tell him? What do you need to know from him?

In this way, you can clearly brief the designer or writer. Then you will get what you want. Beware of clever designers who cannot communicate. They may be concerned with the eye, but you are concerned with the mind.

Chapter Seven

How to Control Costs

Marketing costs, of course, will figure in your overall budget of costs. What you spend on advertising must be recovered by price. Ultimately, it is paid for by your customer or client, unless you fail to achieve profitable sales.

Promotional costs are part of price. Remember that. They do not come out of profits. They should not be based on "what you can afford" other than as a legitimate investment in making a profit. They have to be seen alongside all other costs, such as the purchase of goods for resale, office administration, packing, salaries, overhead, and so on. Promotion is just one item in the total budget.

The question is how to control costs, in order to deliver the greatest return from the least expenditure. Here are some essential areas to consider:

1. *Postage:* This is a major cost, and there are several ways by which it can be controlled.

2. *Number of items:* What is the minimum necessary number?

3. *Weight of items:* Is, for instance, your paper selection correct?

4. *Print costs:* Sound print buying is essential to cost control.

5. *Quantity of mailing:* Selective use of mailing lists, and how they are obtained and maintained, is crucial.

6. *Media buying:* This applies where media other than direct mail and mail drops are used. It involves use of media research data.

You've probably already observed that postage, quantity and print costs are interrelated. Now we will consider how you can get the most out of your dollar in all six areas.

POSTAGE

There are only two ways to keep postage costs down: controlling the weight of the mailer and taking advantage of more economical mailing classifications.

Generally speaking, your pieces may be mailed in two types of categories: first and third class. The two differ in both price and time of delivery. First class may be used by the direct marketer when the goal is to avoid a "just-like-all-the-others" appearance (in other words, to resemble mail the recipient will consider "standard" correspondence). Third class mail costs less to mail in bulk, has a longer delivery time, and is commonly used for printed matter in which no "customization" takes place, and in which each piece is identical to the others in the batch.

As of early 1990, the single piece first class rate was 25 cents for one ounce; presorted first class was 21 cents for the same weight, with various discounts for using the "zip-plus-four" codes (such as Anytown, USA, 00001-2345) and pre-barcoding. Pre-barcoded and presorted first class mail permits are available; good for twelve months, the permits carry a registration fee of $60. The arrangement for third class fees is similar, but certain minimum mailing and sorting restrictions apply.

A number of other important services are offered by the Postal service; for further information, contact the mail requirements room at the central post office in your area.

Payment of postage

Each mailing, of course, requires payment of postage. First class letters are individually stamped or metered (lending them their air of "authenticity"). There are three methods of postage payment for a bulk mailing: the precancelled stamp, the permit imprint, and the postage meter.

The precancelled stamp

The post office issues an authorization number to bulk mail permit holders who wish to purchase precancelled adhesive stamps or precancelled envelopes. There is no additional fee for this type of permit, but authorization from your post office is required.

These stamps or envelopes are recommended for the lower volume bulk mailer, and are purchased at the window section of your post office.

The permit imprint

The permit imprint is in the upper right hand corner of the mailing piece, and features a printed box containing the words "Bulk Rate" and "Postage Paid." The permit imprint must indicate the name of the city and state where the permit is held, and the permit number. There is a one-time non-refundable fee payable at the time you apply for the permit number; this fee is separate from the annual bulk mailing fee.

All pieces must be identical in weight and must be large enough to meet Postal Service guidelines. Other design guidelines apply, as well; your local post office will be able to provide you with all the necessary details.

Meter

There is no licensing fee for using a postage meter, but postal authorization is required, as is the payment of the annual bulk mailing fee. When using meter for bulk rate postage, you will need to use a "Bulk Rate" slug in the imprint mechanism of your meter. Ask your meter supplier for information on obtaining one.

NUMBER OF ITEMS

Exactly how many items are essential? You may gain a new respect for the one-piece mailer when you total up your postal expenditures. Remember, each item represents not only extra weight per piece, but also printing and production outlays. Use only what is necessary to get the job done; do not bombard your recipient with enclosures on principle.

WEIGHT OF ITEMS

What will be the weight of print items? Before ordering printing, ask for paper samples; weigh dummies made up to the sheet size or number of pages of your intended items. Paper can be surprisingly heavy. By experimenting with paper samples, you can decide on the right weight for you. And don't forget to include the weight of the envelope.

The paper size, or number of pages of a catalogue, may have to be considered from the point of view of weight. This can be a critical consideration with overseas mailings. You may find it necessary to use different weights of paper for mailings outside the United States.

PRINT COSTS

Nowadays, modern offset litho printing can offer full-color work at a reasonable cost, but try to get quotes from more than one printer. Prices for the same type of job can vary considerably, due to the use of different machines. Moreover, some printers are more helpful than others in their advice on paper, typography and design. If you can, visit printers and check out what equipment and services they have; this is usually to your advantage. Printers are craftsmen, proud of the skills they offer, and most will be glad to answer your questions.

QUANTITY OF MAILING

What is the most economical quantity for your mailing? This will depend on a combination of mailing list size, cost of postage and envelopes, and printing costs. Once you go on press, the cost for extra leaflets may look attractively economical, but remember: you still have all the other costs to bear.

Quantity will also be related to the sales target. What is the minimum mailing that is likely to achieve the sales target and avoid overexpenditures? When you see some of the blanket mailings put out by some direct marketers, you might think that cost is ignored. The selectivity of direct mail has been forgotten in too many quarters.

MEDIA BUYING

When press and television are used, it is likely that a direct marketing advertising agency will be necessary. Media planning is based on the use of circulation figures, R.L. Polk readership figures and Nielsen television audience figures. Circulation means audited average net sales over a period, usually six months. Readership means the estimated number of readers, plus their demographic details based on income and occupation. This information is obtained by marketing research surveys.

These statistics can help you or your agency prepare media schedules that will help you address your advertisement to your target audience as economically as possible. Media choices will be based on cost-per-thousand circulation or readership, demographic characteristics and elimination of duplication.

An agency can be helpful with both media planning and creative work. Today, there are agencies specializing in direct response marketing, as well as media independents and creative "à la carte agencies."

You may not be big enough to need an agency, in which case you will have to handle your own media buying. Study the relative abilities of different publications to reach your market, given your media buying budget. Your choice may be based on past experience and research.

Getting the most from your media budget

An excellent idea of what can be involved in careful budgeting was set out in an advertisement from Direct Response Media. It appeared in an issue of *Direct Response*, and is quoted below.

Fifteen important media questions
vital to direct marketers

1. Do you like the idea of paying 5 percent media commission (or even less) instead of the usual 15 percent?

2. Have you established the best size and page position for your advertisements?

3. Do you know the optimum frequency for each publication?

4. Would you like to extend your peak selling seasons?

5. Do you usually pay extra for premium positions?

6. Are you paying the lowest rate for your space?

7. Have you negotiated CPI deals?

8. What can you learn from your competitors' media schedules?

9. Are you taking full advantage of short-term opportunities?

10. How quickly can you weed out non-effective media?

11. What are you learning from A/B tests, regional tests, crossover tests?

12. Are you using the savings from short-term buying to test new media?

13. Are you aware of the new opportunities offered by inserts?

14. Have you seen how effectively television can be used in the direct marketing media mix?

15. Do you want media advice based upon unequalled experience of analyzing consumer response?

You now have some idea of the intricacies involved in budgeting direct response marketing relying on press or television. Clearly, the critical nature and necessity of the media planning budget points to the advantages of using a specialized agency.

Chapter Eight

Envelopes

The envelope is the package; it serves four purposes.

1. It can be printed to identify the sender.
2. It can contain the mailing.
3. It can protect contents.
4. It can ensure delivery.

But does it stop there? Should the envelope be a sort of general package, mute and anonymous, or should it identify and announce the sender?

There are not only contradictory schools of thought here, but also questions of policy, psychology and the tactics of persuasion and promotion.

Whatever you may think about junk mail, most people, whether in a private or business capacity, are curious about the mail. They expect mail and are vexed about delays and late deliveries.

Generally, people hope for something good to arrive in the mail. Few people are more popular than the mailman.

The psychology is very different from that regarding virtually any other form of advertising. Mail can be very personal, so let's consider your own attitude. What do you do when confronted by unopened mail? What would you do if you were sent the piece that you yourself are now contemplating sending out?

It is unlikely that your first move will be to slit open the envelope. The first thing most people want to know is not so much the contents, but who sent it. They go through the newly arrived mail, even study postmarks in the attempt to identify senders. They look at stamps and printed information on the front of envelopes or on the flaps. Then they decide which ones to open first.

People may be influenced by the format of their address or by the shape, size or bulk of the envelope. They can be adept at detecting unwanted junk mail, or be able to spot mail they have been expecting. This behavior is particularly true of domestic mail. Your envelope has to survive this sort of scrutiny if it is to survive and succeed in being opened!

The appearance of the envelope can take three forms:

1. It can be an unobtrusive plain envelope.

2. It can have a simple identification, or a return-to-sender address.

3. It can be designed as part of the total mailing, allowing you to start selling right off the envelope.

Let us consider the three different appearances.

Plain envelopes

A simple standard-size white or manila envelope may suit your mailing; it is certainly economical, and you may not want or need to announce your identity with a printed envelope. (You may decide to rubber-stamp discreet, minimal return-address information on the rear flap.) A quality envelope gives the impression that the contents are important, the sender is important, and the recipient is respected.

There are a number of different reasons for using a plain envelope:

1. You need to make your mailing look like normal business correspondence.

2. You need to retain an element of surprise or curiosity, and do not wish to lose this advantage before the envelope is opened.

3. The cost of a printed envelope is not justified.

4. The final recipient may never see the printed envelope, as with business mail, because the envelope will be opened and discarded by someone else.

Envelopes with a printed name

The typical printed business envelope exudes pride and looks efficient. It is valuable in business correspondence (as distinct from direct response marketing). It quickly identifies mail which may be expected or welcomed, such as replies, orders or payments.

A different situation arises with unsolicited direct mail, which is unexpected and not necessarily welcomed. The printed business envelope in these circumstances can be a turn-off. It will destroy the element of surprise, and invite dismissal without even being opened. You need to be careful about provoking a negative reaction. What reaction can you reasonably expect? Have you already established a relationship of some kind with the recipient? (Is a brochure expected, for instance?)

Custom-designed envelopes

If you use custom-designed envelopes, with color, pictures or a printed message, two things can happen. You can start selling off the envelope. Or you can destroy all interest in the envelope's content.

Reader's Digest mailings are sometimes criticized for their aggressive approach with custom-designed envelopes, but this has not stopped *Reader's Digest* from using its hard-selling tactics, so they must work. What happens? Some people throw the pieces away unopened, but other people who have previously bought from *Reader's Digest* open them because they are satisfied customers. Others may be tempted by the prize offers which, after all, appeal to that dependable primary instinct of greed.

It is easiest to sell off the envelope when:

1. The item has been requested and a coupon in a printed advertisement has been sent in. (You can exploit the anticipation.)

2. The recipient is a regular customer who is interested in your latest offer.

3. There is something novel about the offer, and the envelope can arouse instant attention, interest, curiosity and anticipation. (Prizes are sometimes announced on the envelope.)

Envelope printers display a great deal of ingenuity with all the possible designs, shapes and special types of envelope.

Special types or uses of envelopes

Reply envelopes

A reply envelope may seem to be an elementary component, but can it contribute to response and be more than a courtesy?

You may think it sufficient to have an envelope bearing your address. Of course, you will make sure that it fits into the outer envelope without folding. It may have to be a shape and size that can accommodate the order form or payment card without folding it, perhaps for computer handling reasons.

One way to encourage return is to supply a business reply envelope. People do not always have stamps, and they may want to reply immediately. The convenience of a business reply envelope can encourage return replies.

To avoid problems at your end it may be sensible to print reminders under the flap: "Have you included your check?" "Have you put your full address on your order?" Headaches can be prevented by printing reminders on your reply envelope. If coupons or order forms have blanks set aside for state and zip code, time, misdirected orders and complaints can be avoided.

Envelopes can also carry the order form on the reverse side. This saves an extra print item, and helps to simplify response. A typical example is that used by film processing companies. Very explicit instructions are printed on these envelopes. They can be one-piece mailers, but can also serve as magazine inserts and door-to-door mail drops.

Insert envelopes

Some mailings include other envelopes containing special "persuaders" or prize offers. Be careful not to overload a mailing. Some insert envelopes complicate mailings, are out of character with the rest of the mailing and may even annoy recipients.

Many firms do use sealed envelopes, either plain or printed, as enclosures, but consider very carefully whether this will really work in your case. Copycat mailings are not always wise. Of course, it can be argued that insert envelopes help to overcome the static nature of print by making the recipient do something.

Tear-off flap envelopes

Another device that can be helpful to the recipient and give the recipient a participatory role is the envelope with a perforated deep flap or stub (sometimes called a "bangtail"). This is usually an order form, but it can serve special purposes, such as requesting information about other products or services. This device can also offer "referral" gifts if the recipient turns his friends into your customers.

Transparent and shrinkwrapping envelopes

See-through polythene envelopes are a clean, strong and attractive way of packing large items (such as catalogues). Readers will be familiar with them if they receive magazines by mail. A colorful cover will be visible through the polythene, attracting attention more quickly than when a large buff manila or white envelope is used.

Talk to your local supplier to learn all of the features of the envelopes available for your mailing.

Chapter Nine

Contents of a Mailing

Of course, some contents of mailings have already come under discussion. However, we should consider here each possible item. Discussion about the use of novelty items and gimmicks will be included in this chapter, as well.

The contents of a mailing can consist of combinations of the following:

1. Sales letter.
2. Price list.
3. Order form.
4. Reply envelope.
5. Insert envelope.
6. Discount coupons.
7. Catalogue.
8. Leaflet, folder or broadsheet.
9. Sample.
10. Novelty item or gimmick.

Sales letter

This has been discussed fully earlier in the book; the question now is whether or not to have a sales letter in the first place. A one-piece mailer actually replaces the sales letter; catalogues sometimes contain a printed letter as a bound page, but this lacks credibility and is impersonal.

A sales letter works best when it either outlines the offer or introduces an enclosure. These letters fail if they are too long, tedious or pretentious. Unfortunately, sales letters have become to direct response marketing what news releases have to public relations: bad! Yet this can be the most powerful element in a direct mail piece.

Price list

Some mailings contain a price list with an order form and reply envelope. Many companies such as stationers, stamp dealers, office equipment suppliers, auctioneers, horticultural suppliers and booksellers circulate a price list (as opposed to an illustrated catalogue). But it may also be included with the other contents of a mailing. A sales letter may direct attention to new lines or special offers. A price list may be a single sheet of paper, a folder or even a wire-stitched booklet.

Order form

An order, enrollment or proposal form may be a separate sheet, a page in a price list or catalogue, a panel in a one-piece mailer, or a deep detachable flap on the reply envelope. You must decide which is most convenient to both you and your customer, and what method helps contribute the most to achieving the desired level of response within your cost parameters.

There are several important considerations here that concern the planning of the mailing. It may be a good idea to design your piece in such a way that the customer can retain a copy of the order (part of a contract); there may be legal requirements, such as a place to state the age of the respondent. The form should be foolproof in making the customer responsible for placing a clear order that can be executed correctly, so no dispute can arise.

An order form calls for copywriting skills just as much as the sales letter or sales literature. What exactly does the customer want? What exactly do you need? Both requirements have to be satisfied.

Ambiguity can creep in, so be careful. I once made the mistake of offering a choice of three items out of four, with the word "or" between the last two choices. The choice could have been "blue, red, green or white." A number of people sent in money without making a choice because they had missed the word "or." The choice could not be made for them. You can see now why it is good practice to provide boxes that can be marked to indicate choice, and to be crystal clear in both your wording and layout. People are very careless about filling in forms, but the problems that arise may be your fault if you do not provide a guiding hand. Never take anything for granted! Always make directions simple for people to follow.

Reply envelopes

This is a courtesy, and a way to create action. (These envelopes also make sure that people reply to the right address.) Reply envelopes were discussed in detail earlier in the book.

Sealed envelopes as enclosures

Also discussed in previous pages. Do these add extra interest? Arouse curiosity? Place emphasis on some key aspect of the mailing? Give the recipient something to do? Or are they a nuisance? Can the reaction on opening the extra envelope be an anticlimax? Beware: you can extend your welcome with this device, or ruin it.

Some insert envelopes are banal, and underestimate the intelligence of recipients. If a financial firm is sending out an annual report, statement of account or dividend/interest summary, it may be advantageous to accompany this with a new offer contained in a sealed envelope. Doing so implies that the material is important and separate from the main object of the mailing. Moreover, it is contained with something expected or received regularly. This approach may even be a better way of piggybacking on a regular mailing, such as a gas, electricity or telephone account, although in such cases the envelope must be a small one.

Discount coupon

A discount coupon may be a means of getting quick response. Under this heading can also be included premiums and incentives to buy, submit a larger order, enroll a friend or supply addresses. Some of these incentives might include:

1. Speed premiums (when a closing date is given for the offer).

2. Order-increase incentive (when gifts, discounts and/or free shipping are offered to orders over a certain volume or price).

3. Sales leads (when a gift is offered if a coupon is returned—for instance, from a magazine advertisement—or further information, catalogues or quotes are requested).

4. Loss leaders (when items in catalogues are offered at reduced prices—probably at cost—to encourage purchase of regular priced items).

5. Mystery gifts offered for prompt orders (but beware—these should not be so trivial that they invite derision).

6. Gifts for recommendations (when customers are invited to enroll members or supply names of possible customers).

7. Two-step gift leads (when a gift is offered if one offer is accepted, but a better gift is offered if a second, more expensive, offer is accepted).

8. Continuity incentives (like those of some tape and compact disc clubs, who may offer a second product at a bonus price, and a free one if a certain number of purchases are made).

Catalogue

This may be the sole item using a transparent envelope, or may be accompanied by a separate introductory sales letter, as well as other items, such as a reply envelope. The catalogue itself can serve as virtually a one-piece mailer complete with order form; the order form can be perforated and bound within the catalogue, or folded and tucked in with a business reply envelope.

Leaflet, folder or broadsheet

Sales literature may accompany a sales letter, especially when it is to illustrate the offer(s), or to give more detailed information. However, it is best not to clutter the mailing with too many pieces of print. A broadsheet that folds out to form a large display sheet can be a dramatic way of presenting a variety of items, forming, in effect, a simple catalogue.

Free samples

Some products lend themselves to samples if they are flat and do not bulk the envelope. Color swatches, sachets or specimens can give the recipient a realistic idea of the real thing. In addition, this device has been used by fashion houses, coffee producers and paper makers. Publishers send specimen copies or dummies of publications when selling space. Miniature publications have been used effectively to sell both advertisement space and reader subscriptions.

Novelty item or gimmick

Here, ingenuity can be used to attract attention and give the recipient something to do.

A major media publication once attracted interest in its advertisement space with a thin rectangular enclosure. On it was printed an instruction to place the object in water and watch it expand, just as an advertiser's sales would if he advertised in the publication! The object expanded into a functional sponge.

Scratch cards are also popular gimmicks. They often resemble bingo cards or slot machines. Others come in the form of birthday cards with tabs that reveal discounts when pulled, sealed cards that reveal matching pieces when three sides are torn off, cards with tear-off pictures to reveal gifts and other high-impact mail insertions.

Perfume and cosmetic promotions can apply fragrances to the mailings. This is done with a specially formulated solution containing micro-encapsulated particles of perfume which can be applied to the printed material. When the area is rubbed, the fragrance is released. The method is pricey, but certainly distinctive.

The gimmick may be a special form of envelope, one-piece mailer, or sealed item. The merit of these devices is that they go beyond the formal sales letter, and win the sender some credit for being different.

Pop-ups and cut-outs can also be amusing, lively and memorable. Some of these convert into usable items like pen and pencil holders, which can stand on a prospect's desk as a permanent reminder of the product or service.

Another device is to encapsulate a flat item in a section of transparent plastic to provide a souvenir or even a coaster.

Imaginative ideas like these may cost a little more, but in the right environment, they can certainly enliven a mailing. Special enclosures add zest and create an atmosphere of curiosity and excitement while providing a buying incentive.

These novelties or gimmicks, however, must be used with care. Don't be stampeded into using something that only cheapens your image or credibility. Employed unwisely, gimmicks can annoy, create suspicion and have a boomerang effect that can destroy an otherwise good offer. If such extra effort is needed to clinch a sale, it may make recipients wonder whether it is such a good offer after all. Why such a hard sell?

A reputable company, or one whose products are known to be excellent, will probably only create sales resistance by using these tactics. For many firms, there is very little to be gained by courting a medicine show image. Many people realize that nothing is free in this world. The gimmick may set off a series of negative questions and conclusions in the minds of prospects: What does the mailer want from them? Are they such naive and gullible suckers that they cannot resist "something for nothing"? When they are invited to "save" it actually means they have to spend!

Consider gimmicks and novelty items carefully before committing to them. A supermarket sells differently from an upscale boutique. It is important to understand the psychology of direct response marketing: you may need to beat the drum, but then again, your product or service may call for something more discreet. It does not always pay to copy other people. Gimmicks are usually used by people who wish to sell quickly in big quantities to a large market. Your efforts may or may not fall into this category.

Advantages of gimmicks

1. They are creative and enliven a mailing.

2. They overcome the static nature of the medium and induce active participation.

3. They arouse curiosity and, if a prize or discount is involved, they appeal to the acquisitive instinct and human greed.

4. They add to the interest of the mailing, attracting attention to the offer.

5. They can produce larger orders (when, for example, they are used in conjunction with incentives).

6. They can be especially effective if you are one of several traders selling similar lines and you want to stand out from the crowd.

Disadvantages of gimmicks

1. They cost money, and will either reduce profits or increase prices. They have to be paid for one way or another, and must be made to work within a given budget, and not for their own sake.

2. They may irritate and produce overkill.

3. They may seem unnecessary if the offer is a good one and should be capable of selling without them, either on its merits or on the reputation of the mailer.

4. They may actually obscure the offer and be a disincentive.

5. Unless they are original, they can be regarded as copycat ideas and suffer from bad feelings toward other people's gimmicks.

Perhaps the best time for you to consider gimmicks is when all else has failed. However, some of our biggest and most successful direct marketers use gimmicks all the time, and not as a stopgap or mop-up ploy. It all depends on what sort of business you run, who your customers are, and the condition of the marketplace in which you work.

Chapter Ten

Catalogues

The catalogue is the epitome of armchair selling. Its history reaches back to the Chicago mail order traders Montgomery Ward and Sears Roebuck, firms that built fortunes supplying Midwestern farmers more than a century ago.

Today, catalogues the size of telephone directories can be replaced by a number of new formats, including videotape and on-line personal computer access. However, the straightforward printed catalogue is alive and kicking. The current tendency is for the big mail order catalogue houses to move towards smaller, more specialized catalogues.

Catalogues really allow for shopping without shops, except that the shop is literally brought into the home or office. This is done pictorially (photography is discussed later on in this book); by printing techniques (including offset litho, which offers great beauty and realism); and copywriting, a special and essential skill.

How well is your catalogue written? Catalogue copywriting excels where sales letter writing so often fails. There are two possible reasons for this. Catalogues have been produced for more than a century. The limited space available for numerous product descriptions demands concise, accurate word-picture writing with foolproof price details. Copywriting for catalogues is a little like writing captions for photographs. The wording has to say what the picture cannot say for itself. The second reason for the success of much catalogue text is that catalogue writing is recognized as copywriting, whereas the majority of sales letter writers indulge what should really be considered bad business letter writing.

Catalogue copy ranges from the exciting to the factual, according to the product and the marketing.

The role of the catalogue

Catalogues can play the following roles:

1. To present merchandise to prospective buyers.

2. To maintain regular mail order sales.

3. To provoke immediate response.

4. To seek retention for future reference and purchase.

Not all catalogues aim to do all four things. Frequency has a lot to do with this. Some catalogues are published annually, and may well be kept until the next one arrives; others are issued perhaps quarterly or monthly, replacing the previous one. There are seasonal catalogues, as well. Catalogues of more instant appeal, like those piggybacked on other mailings (such as bills) are very short-lived.

Claims in catalogue copy

Despite the excellence of much catalogue copy, some incredible claims are made in catalogues widely distributed by well-known traders.

It may be that errors and false statements occur unintentionally. They may arise through lack of vigilance during the copywriting stage, over-enthusiasm about new lines, inadequate knowledge of products, or naive acceptance of claims made by the manufacturer or supplier.

How does catalogue copy get written? Sometimes, very inefficiently! Often, foolish assumptions are made that the information given is reliable. How often does the writer ever actually see, touch, use or have any experience with what he is writing about? Rarely.

Many catalogue writers work from buyers' descriptions, or from sales literature provided by the manufacturer or supplier. It is important to say "supplier," because many of the products in question are foreign imports. They come from countries where advertising ethics are unknown and trade descriptions are flaunted. It is your responsibility to verify claims and evaluate the qualities of such goods. You cannot afford to take anything for granted. If you do you may run the risk of being taken to court under the existing, strictly enforced consumer protection laws.

This problem really is not that surprising. Do people who write book club or record club catalogues ever read the books or listen to the records and tapes they describe so effusively? It is physically impossible for them to do more than read, repeat or polish up the blurbs provided by the publishers and record makers.

Often, using second-hand descriptions as a basis for catalogue material is worse than knowing nothing about the product. I once wrote an entire mammoth catalogue from hundreds of buyers' descriptions typed on filing cards. I did so 200 miles away from the company's office and never saw one piece of merchandise. Needless to say, there were problems. At least when I wrote vacation brochures I had been to the destinations; these days, when I write book catalogues, I know all the books that are described.

If you want to write rapturous descriptions, the color pictures you select should match them. If you write "These bewitchingly beautiful large-flowered bush roses in dazzling colors will be a constant source of delight all summer and autumn long," don't insult the customer by reproducing eight hideous pictures in improbable colors beside the copy.

Charging for catalogues

Should you charge for your catalogues, or for shipping them?

There is magic in the word "FREE." It rarely fails to win responses. The catalogue may well be very costly to produce; some companies refund their catalogue charge if business results. The majority, however, provide copies with no payment expected from the prospect.

Some companies reduce waste by stating in advertisements that recipients of previous catalogues need not request another. Others send out postcards to test whether people want the next catalogue, deleting from mailing lists those who do not reply.

Specialized catalogues and mag-a-logs

A comparatively recent development is the smaller or special interest catalogue, in contrast to the "big book" catalogues of the long-established mail order catalogue firms. They concentrate on lines such as fashion, household or gardening equipment.

Mag-a-logs are an interesting innovation usually addressed to upmarket readers. In this format, there is editorial content interspersed with advertisements offering goods that can be paid for with charge cards.

Trends in catalogue copy

A study of scores of catalogues has shown that the largest, best-established and most successful catalogues contain brief factual copy that avoids using a single adjective. Newer catalogues, however (often those promoting non-essentials and novelty products to affluent buyers) seem to use more flowery copy. This seems to be contradictory, but the fact remains that catalogue copy addressed to better-off buyers is usually more of a "hard sell" than that directed toward working class buyers.

Is the "yuppie" (young upwardly mobile professional) and "woopie" (well off older person) market really more gullible, more susceptible to the banalities of advertising? Or is it that the newer breed of direct response marketers are as bad at writing catalogue copy as the new breed of financial direct marketers are at writing sales letters? There is always the possibility, too, that these copywriters are wrongly advised by agencies more familiar with the print advertising of mass market consumer goods.

Remember: catalogue copy does need to be credible and convincing, and not merely colorful and compelling. My advice is to avoid going overboard, and keep extravagant claims to a minimum in your copy.

Chapter Eleven

Working with the Printer and Typographer

Whether it comes in the form of sales letters, envelopes, leaflets, folders, price lists, order forms or catalogues, you are eventually going to have to buy something from the printer. Learning how to work smoothly with this key vendor, then, is a subject of primary interest. How much do you know about printing and printers? Even if you do use an agency or a direct mail house, you should have a working knowledge of the essentials. Printing is probably the most expensive part of your promotion. Do you get your money's worth? Remember: you are the customer; good print buying is your responsibility.

Fortunately, this is a part of your business you can enjoy and take pride in. Printers are craftsmen you're likely to enjoy working with, provided you make a little bit of an effort to cooperate with them.

Printing has a long history and is constantly changing. You can benefit from recent developments. The quality of typesetting, papermaking and printing has greatly improved; you can obtain excellent print very economically (color printing, for example).

Today, print shops range from huge ones doing contract printing for national newspapers to compact units, often with design studios. Printers still tend to specialize in certain classes of print; you will have to find the printer best capable of producing your kind of work.

It pays to talk to printers (not just salespeople), and to visit them so you can see the plant and discuss your work. A lot depends on the kind of machines they have, and the extent to which they have typesetting, folding, binding, laminating and other facilities. With all the necessary equipment on-site, the printer will not have to farm out parts of your job to outside specialists.

QUOTES

The first step is to invite printing bids. Price variations may result from the way you have described your requirements, but may also depend on what kind of equipment printers have.

When seeking quotes you should be precise about what you want; give the printer the fullest possible information about the job. What quantity do you want? How many colors? What kind and weight of paper? How many pictures? How much copy? What size page? How many pages? What sort of binding? How many and what kind of folds? What delivery date do you want? Some of these things you may not know or understand; that is why it makes sense to talk to printers ahead of time. They will be able to provide expert advice, and a good printer will volunteer ideas or suggest alternatives.

It is not necessary for you to have assembled your entire project before you begin comparison shopping. You may have written nothing, obtained no pictures, and prepared no layout. You might decide simply to make a dummy and estimate the number of pictures and words, with the general shape and size of the piece of print. Ideally, you should be able to give the printer a rough layout and indicate picture areas and the volume of wording. You can photocopy this dummy and send it to different printers so that they can give you quotes as well.

One thing to remember when you send the complete copy to the printer you choose: be sure all the wording is finalized. It can be very costly to make numerous amendments or rewrites. The only corrections to proofs should be of the printer's errors in typesetting, spacing and positioning. Assuming you are not supplying camera-ready copy, your layout and copy should resemble an architect's drawing and a quantity surveyor's specifications. Once again, it pays to visit a printer and talk to him so you are both absolutely clear about the job.

In a short chapter it is not possible to deal with such a subject in great depth, but there are some particular aspects of printing worth special attention. One of these is typography.

TYPOGRAPHY

Some "turnkey" printing operations will provide typographical services as well as printing and binding; however, you may decide to have your work done at an independent typesetting house.

The appearance and legibility of your print is an important part of its ability to communicate your message. It is well worth taking an interest in typography as opposed to just leaving it to the "expert," although his advice should be sought. Of course, you need to know what typefaces he has.

Typography is the art of specifying the style and size of type to turn your wording into print. Between typewritten copy and printed copy lies all the difference in the world.

There are hundreds of different typefaces. Generally speaking, they fall into two groups: display and text. There are also sans serif and serif faces, the first having no short horizontal lines at the top and bottom or ends of strokes. If more than one design of typeface is used, then there should be a harmonious blend.

You will have many typefaces to choose from, although you will find that selections differ in variety and number depending on the firm. Certain popular typefaces like Times are almost universally available. Ask for a copy of the type specimens manual. This will show you the variety of typefaces they have, usually set out in roman, italic and different weight versions. "Weight" means the lightness or boldness of the type. You can then make comparisons and select the right type for you.

You will notice that some types allow more or fewer characters to the line; this affects how many words can be set in a given space. There will be differences in x-height of small letters like "a" and "o". Some of the more decorative types have low x-heights, which makes them less easy to read in small sizes.

A lot of promotional print is set throughout in sans serif for both display lines and panels or columns of text. This is a lazy habit, originating from the small selection of typefaces that used to be available for phototypesetting by litho printers. Sans serif faces give bold displays, but are less legible for small text. Books, for instance, are not set in sans serif. What's more, if you use shiny paper, sans serif faces are often less easy to read than those with serifs, known as text or book faces. But a blend of sans serif display lines and serif text can make an effective contrast.

A designer who specifies sans serif type throughout a job is either ignorant of typography or out of date. If print is being designed for you, make sure you check and approve the typefaces being specified. A lot of cus-tomers don't, and fail to realize that they are sacrificing a vital tool of communication.

There are many beautiful typefaces. If you choose carefully, your print can be given character, legibility and "pull."

Don't spoil your print by using devices that decrease legibility. If you print small areas such as display lines on a color background, don't use such a heavy color that it kills the words.

Similarly, beware of reversing words to read white on a black or colored background. This may be all right for the occasional display panel with a few large words, but small text can be lost if reversed. It may be a pretty design idea, but it can destroy readability. Beware of designers who think in terms of shapes to look at rather than words to read.

Another way to achieve readability is to be generous with white space. Space between lines of copy, space around copy, good margins, and indented paragraphs all help to make your message readable. A free (unjustified) right-hand edge does not help readability; it is a hangover from the days when typewriter settings could not be justified and had to have ragged right-hand edges.

Short paragraphs have a similar effect. Don't bore a reader with great slabs of verbiage. This may mean writing shorter, crisper copy to let some daylight into the layout. Or it may permit the use of larger type. Short paragraphs, sentences and words help to speed up the reading.

It is worth studying catalogues to see how often or seldom the above principles of good typography are practiced. Unfortunately, you're likely to find a majority of cases that ignore them; designers too often usurp the role of typographers. Nicely designed, printed, well-written print is ruined by bad typography that simply plants a volume of words in a given space. Whether it is legible and readable never enters the heads of those designers who do not read but only look.

Typography has been emphasized here because it is the means of communicating quickly, clearly and effectively. This will not be obvious when you look at words produced on a typewriter. You will have to think about how best to present this typescript print. You may even find it helpful to have a little copy set in different typefaces to see how these samples compare.

LASER PRINTING

There are many laser printing packages available to you; the Hewlett Packard Laser Jet Series II is among the most respected printers available.

Laser printing makes it possible to enliven mailings such as sales letters with special effects. Software used in conjunction with these printers make personalization within the text of a letter, unusual layouts, or combinations of different typestyles quite easy.

Laser printing can be applied to personalized reply cards, prize drawing certificates, invoices, and many other applications. The names, figures, choice of typeface and so on are controlled by computer.

PRODUCTION SCHEDULE

If your print work is to be carried out efficiently, you will have to do some scheduling. Delays can involve extra costs.

It is wise to agree to a production schedule with your printer, and see that you both keep to it. Printers (and especially sales representatives) tend to be optimistic about delivery dates. Make sure your required delivery date is well before you need it. If you tell a printer you want a job a week earlier than you really do, it may arrive on time.

A simple production can follow this pattern, where the D-day numbers in the example cover one month:

Production Schedule	
Copy to printer	D-30
Proofs to printer	D-20
Corrected proofs to printer	D-17
Delivery by printer	D-day

This can be revised and adapted to the complexities of your job. It may be necessary to allow for revised proofs and a final OK; color proofs may have to be checked for accuracy of color. The printer may be responsible for packing and posting, or inserts may have to be delivered to another party by a certain date. Deadlines must be fixed to suit the printer's workload and your own planning for mailing, media advertising or mail drop.

PROOFREADING

Proofreading is a chore, but it is your responsibility to see that the job is correctly laid out. If you're less than vigilant, you'll learn how easy it is for errors to slip through. There can be wrong typefaces, sizes, weights or spacing. Wrong captions may appear under pictures. A picture can be upside down or the wrong way around. In litho printing, everything is pasted down, and may be pasted in the wrong place, not centered or spaced improperly. Fortunately, adjustments are easily made before plate-making.

It is easy to read into proofs what you expect to find because you know what you want to see. Modern computerized phototypesetting is very accurate, but a small mistake in a piece can ruin your work. This is why proofs must be read slowly, syllable by syllable, and then reread. It is often a good idea to ask a stranger to read the proofs. It is surprising how often two proofreaders will spot completely different errors!

Do not rewrite proofs; "author's corrections" can be costly and may cause delayed delivery. Get it right before you send copy to the printer. Don't wait to see what it looks like when proofed. This warning is worth repeating because so many print customers never know what they really want until they see what they don't want. Then they wonder why the job turns out to be more expensive than they anticipated. This is a form of budgetary control or common sense.

DESKTOP PUBLISHING

The computer has made it possible for the writing, editing, layout and typography of publications to take place much more quickly and economically than ever before. On-line transmission direct to the printer is another advantage of the computer age. This is quite well established for house journal production, but the same techniques can be applied to the production of catalogues. You may find this option well worth looking into, especially with work that can be repeated with updates, since the original material can be stored on disk.

One such method is the Wordsmith Publishing System, which uses the Apple Macintosh and costs about $6500 including software and laser printer. This system is designed to output direct to Linotron 500, 300 and 100 typesetters via an electronic link with the printer. Fonts, leading (spaces between material) and computer-generated graphics can be set direct on a variety of paper sizes. The actual page make-up software can produce full-color separations as well as display on the screen of the colors used. Drafts of work can be produced in full color on a matrix printer or in higher resolution (black and white only) on the Laserwriter.

Chapter Twelve

Working with the Photographer

Pictures that are too clever, too professional, too unnatural or unrealistic may lack conviction. Do the models in your catalogues, brochures or print promotions look like centerfold models, or like you, your sister, your girlfriend or your mother-in-law? If customers cannot picture themselves using the umbrella or pushing the lawnmower, then they may not think the goods are meant for them. To look at some travel brochures you would think no one over 20 ever went on vacation or took a cruise!

Perhaps you think that is an exaggeration, that you should sell dreams even when promoting a line of brown metal coathangers. But glamorization can go too far; in fact, it can be the end of the sales pitch. Not always, of course. There can be appeals to vanity when an older woman may want to emulate a younger one.

The art of using photography effectively is to remember that the camera is a means of conveying a message, just like a voice, pen, brush, typewriter or word processor. Photographers are like artists; they specialize in certain mediums or subjects. You may need one who specializes in say, fashions, table-top, outdoor scenes, interiors, flowers or children.

Some photographers are fairly versatile, but others are much better at taking one kind of picture than another. It may be a matter of equipment: make of camera, possession of a studio or of special lighting equipment. Another question is delivery. Some photographers will give you contact prints the next day; with others it may take two weeks. What is your deadline for prints or transparencies?

Good photography also depends on your ability to work with the photographer. A professional photographer knows the technicalities and techniques of his trade, but he does not know what you want unless you tell him. That means you must know what you want, and should not just call in a photographer and expect him to get on with the job. That is a reasonable approach if you call a plumber to fix a burst pipe; it will not get you very far if you want to obtain photographs well suited to your purpose.

Photography is a matter of story telling with a camera, not merely the taking of shots to record whatever is happening at the moment. And yours is the story to be told, not the photographer's. Each picture has to be planned. You are the director; think of yourself as in charge of a movie, collaborating with the cinematographer, and not as a passive spectator on the set.

So what precisely do you want to say? Do you know? Have you thought it out, picture by picture, throughout the piece of print? A photographer may think, "This is a nice angle," or, "This lighting effect will be dramatic," but his artistic ideas can be totally irrelevant. Of course, if you use the same photographer a number of times, he will become familiar with the type of pictures you want, and may well offer valuable advice.

For instance, suppose, you are producing a brochure for a conference center. You will know what conference organizers are looking for, and how best your facilities can satisfy their needs. The impressive exterior of your hall may be less important than the audiovisual equipment or special machinery you have installed. A view of the kitchen may be less important than a scene of a thousand delegates eating.

Assess the project from a pictorial standpoint. An empty auditorium or stage, a blank screen or inactive reception area can make the place look like it is being put up for sale. You have to see pictures with the eyes of the eventual beholder.

Try to visualize the pictures that will influence decisions. In other words, come up with a shooting script.

How? That is your decision, not the photographer's. Every picture needs to be planned in two ways:

1. With a written brief, which will resemble the stage directions for a play or the shooting script for a film or video.

2. With a rough sketch of the composition of the picture. The composition will angle the picture to show what is most significant: the control knob, the large windows, the safety device, the immaculate head waiter, whatever it may be.

Composition is all-important, and is the secret of good photography. Take a single subject like a clock. Shall it be photographed face-on and flat, or turned slightly to give a three-dimensional effect?

If you are taking photographs to fit the layout of a page, pictures on the left of the page should be looking inwards, and vice versa; not every subject can be reversed because the existing picture may not accommodate this. (The rule applies to people in pictures, too.) The reader's eye will follow the direction presented to him by a picture, and you don't want the reader's attention wandering off the page. In which direction are the eyes looking?

If you are using color pictures, make sure they really are color pictures. Subjects like flowers or fashions are usually colorful, but all too often, such photos are made up of dull grays, blues, mauves, browns and greens. Yellow, orange and red are often absent. These bright colors need to be introduced; dull colors make a picture recede from the eye, while bold colors bring a picture forward. Black and yellow, for example, or black and orange, are very striking combinations.

Black and white pictures incorporating monochromatic lighting effects, shadows and silhouettes can produce dramatic effects, as well as the powerful inherent contrasts between black and white. (Many of the old black and white films carry more of a visual "punch" than their later color counterparts!)

PEOPLE IN PICTURES

People can add realism and enhance the interest of some pictures, but they can be irrelevant and distracting in others. Using "people," of course, usually means models and model fees. There are some exceptions to this: scenes may include customers as "extras"; a hotel or restaurant shot can be peopled by members of the owner's family or staff.

People do like looking at other people, whether it be a famous personality giving a testimonial, an attractive model, or a model representing a typical user with whom the reader can relate.

You must take into account several considerations in choosing the appropriate model. Do you want a recognizable person who will glamorize the product; or do you want someone who looks natural, homely or "right" for the subject? Do you want to give your mailing an air of femininity, manliness, class, youthfulness, cheerfulness, seriousness or modernity?

Will customers be put off by a model who is nothing like them? Will they be tempted to look at all the pretty models and ignore the goods? Maybe fashion goods will make buyers feel good if they wear clothes like those the youthful models are wearing. However, a scantily-clad model will only look stupid if you are selling annuities.

What the person is doing in the picture can also be important. It may be better to have a rear or side view of a person using a computer, for instance, so the screen is visible. For products like rings or wrist-watches, only fingers or wrists need to be photographed. You will have to choose a model with the right features, hands or arms, and it may not matter whether they are tall, short, thin or fat.

Correct clothing is yet another consideration. In promotional materials these days, we see some oddly dressed people mowing lawns, decorating walls and even using cake mixers. Sometimes it looks as if the same model has simply moved from one subject to another while still wearing the clothes from the previous shoot. Watch the "wardrobe" aspects if you want credible pictures.

SIZE OF OBJECTS

Do your pictures demonstrate the size of products, and is it an advantage that they do? A photograph can give a false impression of size if the product is not associated with some other item for the sake of perspective. Size can be indicated when a small object is placed in the palm of the hand, or held in the fingers, or set beside a familiar object. Tall or large objects can be associated with the human figure to indicate height or bulk.

Your particular project may call for other techniques. Use or enjoyment can be presented pictorially; many a successful advertisement has been framed around a happy customer enjoying a product. If the chair you are selling is meant to be comfortable, show someone relaxing in it. If it is easy to use, show how easily the user can adjust it. Such photos can be much more convincing than any copy you could write.

Chapter Thirteen

Off-the-Page and Inserts

Mail order traders have long used print advertising to sell goods by mail. Many of the advertisers—now and in the past—have been small (even one-man) businesses. Such marketers have been encouraged by publishers eager to sell space; at the same time, the more reputable publishers have sought to avoid complaints from readers and long-term advertisers.

I once served on an advisory committee set up by a weekly family magazine with a multi-million-copy circulation. Two problems had to be confronted. There were unscrupulous advertisers who attempted to foist useless or undesirable products on the public. And there were potential advertisers who did not appreciate the immense pulling power of mail order advertisements, and had neither sufficient inventory nor the ability to handle a huge volume of orders in a short time.

I also coordinated a panel of overseers responsible for monitoring display advertising. It was incredible to me how many disreputable firms tried to sell dubious "cures" and quasi-medical treatments throught the mail. One firm supplied an outline drawing of the human body on which the sufferer marked where it hurt!

The US Postal Service is increasingly vigilant about mail fraud, and many federal, state, and local laws protect consumers. What's more, many in the industry have begun to take a dim view of the abuses related to mail order; it is now difficult to impossible to obtain display advertising in national publications like USA TODAY without supplying sample products, proof of inventory, and so on. The direct response marketer needs to be well aware of voluntary and legal controls when planning an advertising campaign. As the saying goes, there's nothing wrong with advertising, only with advertisers.

Deception may not be intentional on your part, but you do have to be careful not to make ambiguous claims, however innocently. A classic "accidental" mistake from years past, for example, was the omission of a period after the first word in the description "art silk," so that what was really rayon could be misconstrued to mean art, and not artificial silk. Another common error was to refer to raincoats or watches as "waterproof" when "water resistant" was more accurate.

In preparing copy, it is vital to write product descriptions and to make claims that are beyond reproach. By the same token, direct response advertising copy has to achieve immediate response, and by its very nature must be more of a "hard sell" than other advertising (such as point-of-sale displays, where the goods can be inspected and buying decisions can be made deliberately and leisurely).

To buy clothes, tableware, or furniture without prior examination demands great confidence in the supplier. Such faith is inspired partly by the corporate image of the advertiser, but principally by the wording of the advertisement and by its illustrations. Then, too, there is always the danger that people will read into advertisements what they want to read, basing their interpretations on preconceived notions.

For example, one well-known firm offered a free gift of a cut glass vase, and pictured it holding flowers. It was easy for a reader to think in terms of the average vase standing about nine inches tall, and to overlook the fact that the free gift was only three inches tall, or roughly the height of a salt shaker. (The measurement was buried in a paragraph of 60 words.) You must try to think like your reader; blaming the reader for making mistakes won't get you very far.

Similarly, if you are selling furniture or other goods that must be assembled by the consumer, you should explain that your product does have to be put together after purchase. Some people are baffled by the task of assembling things. A dresser I saw advertised recently actually required a *power drill* for assembly.

Advertisements usually show a product already erected, not taken apart and lying flat in a box. Customers buy the article *as shown*, not a kit. You must take nothing for granted, otherwise you will only invite anger and derision.

While some mail-order goods are once-only buys, you may want to build live customer lists and gain repeat business. Only satisfied customers come back again. It is true that you can fool some of the people some of the time, but usually only once. If it is your aim to use media advertising to build lists for direct mail, don't sacrifice goodwill by creating disappointment and mistrust from the very first sale.

It is normal in advertising copy for generalized, emotive language to be used, but in direct response print advertising the wording has to consist of precise word pictures. It is another kind of copywriting altogether, and that is where a specialized direct marketing advertising agency should be strong. Artwork and media buying are not enough.

You can sell all kinds of things through print advertisements, including foreign stamps, collectibles such as coins, insurance, clothes, books, jewelry, furniture, tableware, plants, investment opportunities, charity appeals, and records, to name but a few.

Print media are vitally important when it comes to shaping consumer perceptions. Television has not destroyed the printed word any more than the CD player has destroyed the playing of instruments. For those interested in pursuing its nuances, off-the-page advertising remains one of the most exciting options in direct response today.

Whether or not you decide to use an advertising agency, you will want to review the elements in the next section.

Media

The budget, and its allocation to various media resulting in a planned media schedule of insertions, needs to be prepared at least six months in advance. The actual choice of merchandise and production of creative work may be decided at shorter intervals, depending on copy dates. Lead times will vary from publication to publication.

Ad rates must be judged not just by the rate card, but also by the cost per thousand readers or circulation. In addition, you should consider the demographic characteristics of a publication's readers. Success can also depend on date, position, and size of insertion, and on outside factors like weather and political/economic conditions. A very small advertisement can succeed if it is accompanied by similar ads in a sort of "marketplace" section of the publication devoted to your subject.

The economics of advertising are based on cost per thousand readers or circulation. (These numbers are usually generated and verified by reliable independent sources such as ABC.) The circulation of a given paper may be small when compared to that of another paper, but more people may read each copy of the first than the second. Magazines often found in waiting rooms usually have a high secondary readership, such as *Reader's Digest*. Free newspapers usually have larger circulations than paid-for local newspapers, because of better penetration of a given market. But how many people, on average, read each copy of the free paper? Clearly, you cannot judge by rate alone.

You also have to compare both response and conversion into sales. If you key your advertisements (by printing a date or number on the coupon, such as NYT1 or NYT2 for successive placements in the *New York Times*), you can count the replies to each advertisement. If you divide the number of replies into the cost of the space, you will arrive at the cost per reply.

Each insertion will produce a different result, not just for each publication, but for each date and each different product. Thus, you can discover the most economic medium, the best days or dates, and the most attractive product. You may have to add some value judgments about circumstances that influenced the results.

Cost per conversion can be even more interesting. The insertion that produces the most replies may not produce the most or the best conversions if your ad is aimed at getting catalogue requests. (Of course, the same principle works in reverse: an ad that seems to be performing badly, but that generates high rates of conversion per inquiry, may be worthwhile after all.) The issue of identifying your sales and requests in this way is discussed in the next chapter.

Using these analyses, you (and your agency, if you use one) can arrive at the most economical media list for future campaigns. It is remarkable how publications that seem similar can produce utterly different results; the trick is to spend the least and get the most. You will find that careful research may reveal that it pays to advertise in certain media only on particular dates. Be insistent about this, whatever high-pressure salespeople (or agency personnel, for that matter) say.

Design

This is where your agency can help, especially if you need to illustrate goods, perhaps in color. Your advertisement is your shop window; you are a retailer. The advertisement must be properly "dressed" so that your merchandise is presented as attractively, authentically, and realistically as possible. The reader must be able to see exactly what he or she is being persuaded to buy. (At this point you may want to reread the earlier chapter on photography.)

Laying out pictures and text requires creative skill if the advertisement is to attract attention, arouse interest, create desire, inspire confidence, and provoke action. Remember, an advertisement has to compete for attention, and although print is static, it has to stimulate the eye through words and pictures. The reader must decide, as a result of the ad, to fill in a coupon and mail it.

Copy

The wording must be appropriate to the medium and the reader. What may suit the *National Enquirer* may not suit the *Wall Street Journal*. You may have a lot to say, but make sure that it is not only informational and persuasive, but readable and legible, and that the ad is set out so that the reader is induced to read it.

Short words, short sentences, and short paragraphs; use of white space for clarity or emphasis; avoidance of unfamiliar words; these will all help you get your copy read. If a reader stops at an unfamiliar or incomprehensible word, the flow is halted; you have lost a prospective customer. Nowadays, people do not read; they skip and skim. You may have to keep them reading by using devices like subheadings and italic or bold type. These typographical effects have to be taken into account when the copy is written.

Coupons

The writing of coupons is an art in itself. Make sure that your name and address is printed in the body of the advertisement as well as in the coupon, in case people want it after the coupon has been cut out. This point is often overlooked.

What do you want your customer to tell you? Full name, address, telephone number, job title, sex, age? If a *choice* is to be made, make sure it is easy to state it on the coupon or order form, perhaps with boxes to check off. Alternative choices may be important, so that you can supply without further correspondence if you are out of stock on the first choice. Is there enough *space* for the customer to give you the information you need? Is the coupon well *positioned* so that it is easy to clip? Dot lines and even pictorial scissors inserted in the dot line can help to get the coupon into an envelope and on its way to you.

Coupons are essential in print mail order ads—but even so, you have to ask yourself: will readers take the trouble to clip the coupon? Will they be willing to damage a favorite magazine they're in the habit of keeping? When, exactly, will they cut out a coupon on a text page of, say, *TV Guide*: at the end of the week, if they remember? What about positioning? Coupons have been known to show up on opposite sides of the same page!

One device that can resolve these problems (especially inertia) is the pull-off reply card (typically employing a business reply indicia). Such cards are novel, invite response, need no envelope, and are easily and quickly returned.

As we've noted, coupons can be keyed so that response can be idenified for source, counted and evaluated. Keys can be introduced into addresses by a change of initial if a personal name is used, or by including a room or department number. However, this can depend on people writing the address correctly. A simple method is to print a distinctive key on the coupon, using a different one for each insertion.

Audio and Video Tapes

These are devices that take your spoken or visual message right into the home or office. (An audio tape can even be played back in the car.) Such tapes have been offered to great success by many companies in promotional campaigns.

Inserts

The attractions of inserts are that they allow you to say more than in an advertisement space, and they cost less than advertisement space. They are widely used in magazines. One direct response agency handles 200 million inserts a year. But a large print run is necessary, and there can be problems with waste.

Like junk mail, inserts can be resented. Some readers automatically toss inserts into the wastebasket before reading a publication. Inserts can be a nuisance. And yet one finds the same advertisers repeatedly using inserts, and claiming that they save postage; they piggyback onto the large circulations of magazines and newspapers that penetrate just the right market.

Inserts certainly carry their share of pros and cons. Let's look at the good and bad points in detail, and see exactly how inserts can be made to work for you.

Survival

Not only are inserts likely to be discarded; their life is not likely to extend beyond the original reader. An advertisement in the same publication, however, will continue working as long as the copy of the journal is around. There can be short-term response from an insert compared with long-term response from a display advertisement. By the same token, a reader sufficiently interested to extract the insert is probably a good candidate to mail in the coupon, or retain the insert for further reference.

Size

The size and shape of an insert may translate into interest. If it is similar in format to the page of the publication in which it is found, it may be retained because it seems to be part of the issue. If it is of smaller size or different in shape, it will stand out more obviously as a tip-in.

The hit-or-miss effect

Perhaps it is a delusion that inserts are a waste of money because so many people throw them away. If only the occasional reader takes an interest and responds, that's generally considered good business. Do all the thousands of readers of newspapers and magazines read every advertisement? More selective though it may be, does direct mail have large percentage response? By way of comparison, remember that it can be quite economical to mail 5000 shots to get 50 orders, if the product is of substantial value. It all depends on what it costs to make a sale. When it comes to inserts, that cost may still be a tiny fraction of the selling price.

Unavoidability

Inserts thrust themselves upon readers; you might say they fall into readers' hands more effectively than many other media. They are intrusive, begging for attention, whether discarded or not, and thus present an advantage over the fixed, more static display advertisement.

Selectivity

Especially with "controlled circulation" journals, it is possible to limit insertions to copies sent to particular groups of readers. Except with regional or international editions, it is generally not possible to limit advertisements to certain readers. This restricted use of inserts can be used to test response. In the case of some publications, it is possible to direct inserts by zip-code, a powerful marketing advantage for those who want to target key demographic groups.

The best-available-alternative factor

Very often, inserts are used for lack of something better and because the cost of space advertising is prohibitive. Usually, this means lack of a good mailing list. In other words, inserts can be the poor man's alternative to direct mail.

Chapter Fourteen

How to Research and Record Results

KEYING

It is necessary to identify the response source in order to determine the efficiency of any medium. This may appear easy at first, especially if the response comes primarily or exclusively from an annual or seasonal catalogue. As we will see in this chapter, however, things are not always that simple.

It really is surprising how often people keep old material and order from it months (or years!) later. You may recognize the order form from last fall's catalogue, but will you be able to tell when someone places a phone or mail order based on this older sales literature? Your only clue may be a price or stock change on the item in question.

Some magazines have remarkably long lives, and customers may send you orders in response to old off-the-page advertisements. Of course, source identification becomes even more important if you advertise frequently.

There are a number of simple ways to approach the issue of identification. You may not want the customer to be involved at all, or even be aware that you are conducting a check. It is possible to skew results by being too blatant about these devices; if the customer spots your keying method in two advertisements and decides to use the key in what is thought to be the more important medium, the visibility of the other medium may be understated. It's not uncommon, for instance, when the same ad runs in both national and regional publications, for the national ad's coupons received from a given area to greatly outnumber those received from the regional paper, though, within the area in question, both ads were seen by consumers. (The repetition may, of course, have been useful in reinforcing interest.)

Here are some methods of keying. You will have to decide which is the most appropriate for your business.

1. If a real or imaginary name is included in the address, it can be varied for each medium or insertion. People are generally careful to give the correct address when they want something. Similarly, reply envelopes can be sorted according to key, and attributed to each source. For a campaign consisting of advertisements in numerous newspapers, I once used my own name in the address—but altered the initial 26 times, from A. Jefkins to Z. Jefkins. It made identification very easy.

2. If you want to know the areas of the country from which replies come, you can retain and sort the envelopes by town. This can reveal the volume of response from the various areas; with such information, you can determine which areas warrant more effort in the future, which should be eliminated from your schedule, and which require more attention immediately. Reply envelopes can be a rich source of ready-made in-house research.

3. Keys can be printed discreetly on coupons, showing which insertion in which publication produced the response and when.

4. Serial numbers can be printed on all kinds of materials, such as prize coupons and order forms. You can determine which series of numbers (perhaps with prefixes) is used each time.

5. Different colored return items can be used in succeeding mailings. You can use a different color for ink or paper. Color coding can be applied to reply envelopes or cards, coupons, or order forms. This can be very useful with piggybacked mailings. If, for example, you were piggybacking on gas and electricity bills, you could use one color insert for gas and one for electricity.

6. Different tyopography is another way of identifying response. One item may be printed in sans serif type and another in serif type; the distinction will identify response.

When your incoming mail is researched in these ways you can make your promotional efforts more efficient, and produce the answers to the following questions:

1. Which publications should be used for future advertising?

2. Which dates or days of the week produce the best response and which the worst?

3. Where do the responses come from geographically?

4. How much does each inquiry cost you?

5. How much does each order resulting from an inquiry cost you?

You can go further and analyze the responses themselves—especially orders. If you use a personal computer to record inquiries and orders, you can apply appropriate searches. Thus, you can learn important information about the respondents:

1. Male or female

2. Age

3. Position

4. Location

5. Item(s) purchased

6. Value of order(s)

7. Repeat buyers

8. Non-repeat buyers

This data can help in producing future media schedules; maintaining databases and mailing lists; the use of geodemographic targeting; and merchandise selection.

MEDIA AND COPY TESTING

You may plan an off-the-page advertising campaign; but how do you choose the right publications? You can compare rates on publishers' rate cards, study circulation and readership figures, or examine demographic profiles. Much of this information can be reviewed during a visit to the business section of your public library; other data will require contact with the advertisers or with an advertising agency, if you use one. An agency can pull all the facts together, put it into a comprehensible format, and propose a media schedule.

But there is still no guarantee that *Penthouse Letters* will be more effective and economical than *The Wall Street Journal*. One way to become a little more secure about your decision is to have split runs, or to use regional editions of national publications. There are two main methods to consider.

The a/b split method

This entails printing a control and a test advertisement in different copies of the same publication, on the same day and in the same position, and comparing the results. Similarly, you can do this with different radio and TV stations. (You may even be able to try running different spots simultaneously on the same station, but this is likely to be complicated and prohibitively expensive.)

The crossover test

Run different ads in different journals; then switch the ads for two more issues of these two journals.

Copy testing can also be conducted by traditional door-to-door or on-the-street interviewing, in which a sample of prospects is asked to study and recall parts of a series of proposed advertisements. Different research firms follow various techniques on this score. The approaches vary from the folder method, in which different advertisements are displayed one by one, to the reading, noting, and recall tests, in which respondents are asked what they remember of an advertisement that appeared the previous day. These and other types of copy testing can help to eliminate bad points or enhance or vary other elements in the layout or copy. However, if willingness to buy is registered, you do have to allow for the fact that the advertisement was seen in isolation. When the advertisement eventually appears, willingness to buy may not necessarily be translated into actual purchase.

Nevertheless, these kinds of research can be valuable in perfecting advertisements and avoiding costly mistakes. The people who create ads may be clever, but tested reactions may produce some surprising results. The creators may think they are right; you may choose what you believe to be the best copy and presentation; but if the consumer response is negative, the ad will not be effective, and both you and the creative people will be wrong. Remember: you can be too clever sometimes. Some prize-winning advertising campaigns have been failures in the marketplace.

Ten golden rules of testing

In an excellent brochure on the topic, *Direct Response Media* offers the following sage advice on testing:

1. Remember, test results do not necessarily translate between companies, products, media, seasons, and so on.

2. Test the big issues first: those whose outcome is likely to have the greatest bearing on your objectives.

3. Never believe a single test result. Repeat important tests at least three times or more.

4. Never forget a test result. Keep a "bible" of results and refer to it often.

5. Test market variables over style of copy. In other words, test product, price, proposition, and premium before testing words, pictures, and layout.

6. Keep an eye out for other people's tests and try to piece together their conclusions.

7. Never forget a test opportunity. There is always a question someone in your organization would like to have answered.

8. Progress advertisement by advertisement and not campaign by campaign; allow yourself to be influenced by test results only as they become conclusive.

9. Remember: inexpensive tests are often the most fruitful.

10. Do not let testing atrophy your judgment: you will need judgment to know what to test.

COLOR TESTING

You probably have a favorite color or colors. But do your customers share your preferences? Do they react favorably or unfavorably to the colors you select? We've already addressed the problem of a muddle of items being present in a mailing; there can also be a muddle of conflicting colors.

Color has a language and a psychology. It is an issue that must be considered closely, especially if you are exporting. In some countries black is the color for mourning, while in others it is white. In Asiatic cultures, pale blue is a sad color. Muslims tend to like green, while Chinese love red and gold.

Some colors, like red and orange, leap out at you, while pastel shades like mauve recede. Young people (especially children) like red. Yellow tends to reflect hope and happiness, while green can appeal to go-getters.

Obviously, there are some generalizations here, but you may find it useful to include color in your testing. What response do you get to the use of different shades? Which color is best if you want to be conservative? Abrasive? The bearer of good news? Which are the best seasonal colors? (You might settle on yellow in the spring, blue in the summer, brown in the autumn, and red in the winter.)

PRICE TESTING

It will come as no surprise to learn that the price you charge may have a significant effect on your sales. But which price will produce the maximum sales revenue for you?

Some goods sell because they are bargains; others because a high price carries a sense of status. People often judge quality by price. A British firm that produced excellent watches failed to establish any presence in the marketplace because the watches were underpriced, and suspicious consumers stayed away.

Don't be afraid of price: it often has a great deal to do with the consumer's eventual satisfaction. It is surprising what people will pay if they think the price is right. Is a Rolls-Royce "worth" four times the price of an average good car? If you own one, odds are that you feel confident that the price was right. But if you don't?

In direct response marketing, it is possible to test price by conducting sample mailings of the same product at different prices to find out which one pulls the most sales. The variation in price may be slight, and you alone cannot always assess the right price. The issue is complicated, and more than just a matter of adding a percentage point to your costs. A dollar in either direction can make all the difference.

OFFER TESTING

This involves testing either the merchandise or the proposition. Once again, samples of the prospect list can be tested or, as discussed earlier, split run and regional editions can be used to test alternative products.

As we have seen, getting the offer right is essential. But how far do you rely on your buying and promotional skills, and how often do you actually put products to the test before committing significant amounts of money?

Offer testing also encompasses free gifts and other devices to stimulate action. Are the frills really necessary? Can the merchandise sell on its own merits? Does a gift invite doubt about the offer? It's worth testing these alternatives—the straight proposition and the addition of some gimmick or freebie.

In testing, two rules have to be obeyed. First, the sample must be large enough to be representative of typical customers. Second, if you normally sell nationally, the test including the medium used, must be a miniature of the broadscale market.

Below are selected list brokers you may wish to contact in setting up your mailing campaign.

ADCO LIST MANAGEMENT
Subs. of Alan Drey Co., Inc.
600 Third Avenue
New York, NY 10016
Telephone: (212) 661-0440

ADVANCED MANAGEMENT SYSTEMS, INC.
9255 Sunset Blvd./Penthouse
Los Angeles, CA 90069
Telephone: (213) 858-1520, (212) 967-2711

ADVANCED TECHNOLOGY MARKETING, INC.
5800 Hannum Avenue
Culver City, CA 90230
Telephone: (800) 624-4303

AFFINITY MARKETING GROUP
156 Fifth Avenue (Suite 231)
New York, NY 10010-7002
Telephone: (212) 463-7290

AGGRESSIVE LIST MANAGEMENT, INC.
3231 N. Wilke Road, Suite 3111
Arlington Heights, IL 60004
Telephone: (312) 577-4455

ALDATA LIST MANAGEMENT SERVICES
7300 W. 147th Street (Suite 500)
Apple Valley, MN 55124
Telephone: (612) 432-6800, (800) 331-4710

ALM CO.
501 Great Circle Road
Nashville, TN 37228
Telephone: (615) 248-6166

AMERICAN BABY DIRECT MAIL
Cahners Publishing/Div. of Reed Publishing USA
249 W. 17th Street
New York, NY 10011
Telephone: (212) 337-7167

AZ LIST MANAGERS
Subs. of AZ Marketing Services Inc.
31 River Road
Cos Cob, CT 06807
Telephone: (203) 629-8088

BAK MANAGEMENT
247 Mill Street
Greenwich, CT 06830
Telephone: (203) 531-0033

BURLINGTON MARKETING
14 Vincent Road
Burlington, MA 01803
Telephone: (617) 272-3432

BUSINESS MAILERS, INC.
Subs. of Macmillan, Inc.
640 N. LaSalle Drive
Chicago, IL 60610
Telephone: (312) 943-6666

ELAINE CANTER INC.
675 Mamaroneck Avenue
Mamaroneck, NY 10543
Telephone: (914) 381-2010, FAX: (914) 381-2163

CMP PUBLICATIONS
600 Community Drive
Manhasset, NY 11030
Telephone: (516) 562-5000, (800) 645-6278 x3848

COMPUTER DIRECTIONS GROUP, INC.
345 Park Avenue South, 8th floor
New York, NY 10010
Telephone: (212) 685-4600

COOLIDGE LIST MARKETING
Subs. of The Coolidge Co., Inc.
25 West 43rd Street, 12th floor
New York, NY 10036
Telephone: (212) 642-0310

CROMWELL LISTS/DIV DRI
Affiliate of Leichtung
4944 Commerce Parkway
Cleveland, OH 44128
Telephone: (216) 831-6193

CUSTOM LIST SERVICES, INC.
3 Metro Plaza, Suite 107,
8300 Professional Place
Landover, MD 20785
Telephone: (301) 459-9885

DATABASE MANAGEMENT
Div. of Computer Directions Group, Inc.
345 Park Avenue South
New York, NY 10010
Telephone: (212) 685-4600

DIRECT COMMUNICATIONS CORP.
75 Main Street
Fair Haven, VT 05743
Telephone: (802) 265-8144

DIRECT MEDIA LIST MANAGEMENT GROUP, INC.
70 Riverdale Avenue, P.O. Box 4565
Greenwich, CT 06830
Telephone: (203) 531-1091

DOUBLEDAY MAILING LISTS
Subs. of Doubleday Book and Music Clubs, Inc.
501 Franklin Avenue
Garden City, NY 11530
Telephone: (516) 294-4065

DSI LIST MANAGEMENT
Div. of Demographic Systems
325 Hudson Street
New York, NY 10013
Telephone: (212) 929-1519

MAL DUNN ASSOCIATES, INC.
Hardscrabble Road
Croton Falls, NY 10519
Telephone: (914) 277-5558

ELSEVIER BUSINESS LISTS
Div. of Gordon Publications, Inc.
P.O. Box 1952
Dover, NJ 07801
Telephone: (201) 361-9060

ENTERPRISE LISTS
Div. of Enterprise Publishing, Inc.
725 N. Market Street
Wilmington, DE 19801
Telephone: (302) 654-0110

FDR LIST MANAGEMENT
Div. of Flynn Direct Response, Inc.
62 Spring Hill Road
Trumbull, CT 06611
Telephone: (203) 452-1919

GEORGE-MANN ASSOCIATES, INC.
50 Lake Dr., P.O. Box 930
Highstown, NJ 08520
Telephone: (609) 443-1330

HEARST BUSINESS LISTS RENTALS
Div. of Hearst Business Communciations, Inc.
645 Stewart Avenue
Garden City, NY 11530
Telephone: (516) 227-1300

HINER & ASSOCIATES, INC.
3606 Forest Drive
Alexandria, VA 22302
Telephone: (703) 379-2400

HOUSEHOLD TARGETING, INC.
One Lincoln Plaza, 5th Floor
New York, NY 10023
Telephone: (212) 362-8500

HVB LIST PROMOTIONS, INC.
P.O. Box 6724
Annapolis, MD 21401
Telephone: (301) 261-8652

JAMI MARKETING SERVICES, INC.
2 Executive Drive
Fort Lee, NJ 07024
Telephone: (201) 461-8868

THE KAPLAN AGENCY, INC.
11 Forest Street
New Canaan, CT 06840
Telephone: (203) 972-3600

L H MANAGEMENT DIV.
Div. of Leon Henry, Inc.
455 Central Ave., Suite 315
Scarsdale, NY 10583
Telephone: (914) 723-3176

LISTCO MAILING LISTS
315 W. 58th Street
New York, NY 10019
Telephone: (212) 765-8547

LISTS INTERNATIONAL, INC.
Subs. of Accredited Mailing Lists Inc.
3 Park Avenue
New York, NY 10016
Telephone: (212) 889-9580

MADISON DIRECT MARKETING LTD.
295 Madison Avenue
New York, NY 10017
Telephone: (212) 370-5009

MAIL MARKETING, INC.
171 Terrace Street
Haworth, NJ 07641-1899
Telephone: (201) 387-1010

MARKETING SERVICES INTERNATIONAL, INC.
625 N. Michigan (Suite 1920)
Chicago, IL 60611-3111
Telephone: (312) 642-1620

MCRB
11633 Victory Blvd.
North Hollywood, CA 91609
Telephone: (213) 877-5384

M/D/A LIST MANAGMENT, INC.
Subs. of Mal Dunn Associates, Inc.
Hardscrabble Road
Croton Falls, NY 10519
Telephone: (914) 277-5558

MEDEC LIST MARKETING
Div. of Medical Economics Co.
680 Kinderkamack Road
Oradell, NJ 07649
Telephone: (201) 262-3030

MEDIA MARKETPLACE, INC.
6 Penns Trail, P.O. Box 500
Newtown, PA 18940-0500
Telephone: (215) 968-5020

MEDIA MASTERS, INC.
Subs. of Target Mailing Lists, Inc.
205 Lexington Avenue
New York, NY 10016
Telephone: (212) 696-1321

MEREDITH LIST MARKETING
Locust at 17th
Des Moines, IA 50336
Telephone: (515) 284-2891

MGT ASSOCIATES, INC.
4676 Admiralty Way (Suite 421)
Marina del Ray, CA 90292
Telephone: (213) 822-4911

MILLER MARKETING, INC.
10 E. 39th Street (Suite 1115)
New York, NY 10016
Telephone: (212) 685-6211

MPG LIST CO.
111 Oronoco Street
Alexandria, VA 22314
Telephone: (703) 683-3635

THE NAME BANK
Div. of Agora, Inc.
824 E. Baltimore Street
Baltimore, MD 21202
Telephone: (301) 234-0515

NAME-FINDERS LISTS, INC.
2121 Bryant, #304
San Francisco, CA 94110
Telephone: (415) 641-5208, (800) 221-5009

NATIONAL DIRECT MARKETING
105 N. Main Street
Rockford, IL 61101
Telephone: (815) 963-8136

NCRI LIST MANAGEMENT
Div. of National Consumer Research Inc.
45 Legion Drive
Cresskill, NJ 07626
Telephone: (201) 894-8300

NETWORK PUBLICATIONS
Div. of ETR Associates
#4 Carbonero Way
Scotts Valley, CA 95066
Telephone: (408) 438-4060

P&L DIRECT MARKETING GROUP
3599 Cahuenga Blvd., West
Los Angeles, CA 90068
Telephone: (213) 850-0400, (212) 967-2711

PHILLIPS PUBLISHING, INC.
7811 Montrose Road
Potomac, MD 20854
Telephone: (301) 340-2100

PRESTIGE MAILING LISTS, INC.
1539 Sawtelle Blvd. (Suite 1)
Los Angeles, CA 90025
Telephone: (213) 473-7116

QUALIFIED LISTS CORP.
Div. of The Walter Karl Companies
135 Bedford Road
Armonk, NY 10504
Telephone: (914) 273-6606

RIFFKIN DIRECT, INC.
64 Appletree Lane
Roslyn Heights, NY 11577
Telephone: (212) 463-8955, (516) 621-1076

RMP MANAGEMENT
Div. of Response Media Products, Inc.
2323 Perimeter Park Dr. (Suite 200)
Atlanta, GA 30341
Telephone: (404) 451-5478

ROMAN MANAGED LISTS, INC.
20 Squadron Blvd. (Suite 650)
New City, NY 10956
Telephone: (914) 638-2530, (800) FAB-LIST, FAX:
(914) 638-2631

SAAVOY LISTS
277 Forest Avenue
Paramus, NJ 07652
Telephone: (201) 967-5777

GARY SLAUGHTER CORP.
Div. of Trinet
7970 Old Georgetown Road
Bethesda, MD 20814
Telephone: (301) 986-0840

THOMAS LIST MARKETING
Subs. of Thomas Publishing Co.
One Penn Plaza
New York, NY 10119
Telephone: (212) 290-7224

HARRY TURNER & ASSOCIATES INC.
1515 N.W. Saline
Topeka, KS 66618
Telephone: (913) 357-5000

21ST CENTURY MARKETING
2 Dubon Court
Farmingdale, NY 11735
Telephone: (516) 293-8550

US WEST COMMUNICATIONS
Subs. of U.S. West
1005 17th St. (Room 1290)
Denver, CO 80202
Telephone: (303) 896-6478

WARREN, GORHAM & LAMONT, INC.
Subs. of International Thompson Organization
1 Penn Plaza, 42nd Fl.
New York, NY 10119
Telephone: (212) 971-5000

WMI/WORLDATA
500 N. Broadway
Jericho, NY 11753
Telephone: (516) 931-2442

ZIFF-DAVIS PROFESSIONAL LIST SERVICES
Div. of Ziff-Davis Publishing Co.
One Park Avenue
New York, NY 10016
Telephone: (212) 503-5394

Bibliography

Baier, Martin. *Elements of Direct Mail Marketing*. New York: McGraw-Hill, Inc., ©1983.

Burnett (Ed.). *The Complete Direct Mail List Handbook*. Englewood Cliffs, N.J.: Prentice-Hall, ©1988.

Colter, William A. *Direct Response Marketing*. New York: Wiley & Sons, ©1984.

Fraser-Robinson, John. *The Secrets of Effective Direct Mail*. London: McGraw-Hill, ©1989.

Lewis, Herschell Gordon. *Direct Mail Copy That Sells*. Englewood Cliffs, N.J.: Prentice-Hall, ©1984.

Posch, Robert J. *The Direct Marketer's Legal Adviser*. New York: McGraw-Hill, ©1989.

Rockmorton, Joan T. H. *Winning in Direct Response Advertising*. Englewood Cliffs, N.J.: Prentice-Hall ©1986.